COLORADO'S
CARLINO
BROTHERS

COLORADO'S CARLINO BROTHERS

A BOOTLEGGING EMPIRE

SAM CARLINO

THE
History
PRESS

Published by The History Press
Charleston, SC
www.historypress.com

Cover images: Pete Carlino (*left*) and Sam Carlino mugshots. *Courtesy of the Carlino family collection.*

First published 2019

Manufactured in the United States

ISBN 9781467143271

Library of Congress Control Number: 2019945061

Notice: The information in this book is true and complete to the best of our knowledge. It is offered without guarantee on the part of the author or The History Press. The author and The History Press disclaim all liability in connection with the use of this book.

"Being the grandson of the Colorado Mafia chief, Mr. Carlino brings a fresh perspective to the relationship of the Colorado Mafia and the powerful New York syndicate chiefs."

—Dr. Humbert Nelli, Professor Emeritus, University of Kentucky, author and mafia historian

"*Colorado's Carlino Brothers*...is at once an intimate family portrait and a detailed Mafia history. The author deftly tracks the development of the regional crime family before and through the Prohibition Era, revealing its proper place in the national scene, while providing personal insight into his ancestors."

—Thomas Hunt, author and mafia historian

"The Carlino family already had an amazing history in San Jose, but it was jaw-dropping to discover the family's Colorado story. Sam Carlino's painstaking research paints a realistic and sometimes frightening picture of what life was like in Prohibition-era Colorado. It's the immigrant story, Americana and true crime wrapped up in one package."

—Sal Pizarro, *San Jose Mercury News*

"In the wild West, a bootlegging family enterprise is forced to simultaneously fight off the Feds and Mafia, ultimately to no avail. It reads like a novel, except it's all true!"

—Dr. Larry Gerston, PhD, Professor Emeritus, San Jose State University

I dedicate this book to my father, Sam Carlino,
and his brothers, Vic, Joe, Chuck, Steve and Pete.

You lived it.

Contents

CONTENTS

Foreword

Newspapers of the 1920s and 1930s and the Gentile memoirs first published in 1963 revealed that the Pueblo and Trinidad area of southern Colorado was home to an influential and powerful criminal society with strong connections to mafia organizations in New Orleans, Los Angeles, Kansas City and elsewhere. According to these sources, mafia leaders across the country concerned themselves with the Pueblo area's underworld events and involved themselves in its disputes. These facts should not have been overlooked, but they were.

Fortunately, some historians have worked to recover that old fumble. In the 1970s, Humbert Nelli drew some attention to Colorado's mafia. This occurred as he tried to determine if there was any historical basis for the legend of Charlie Luciano's 1931 purge of old-line Mafiosi (the so-called Night of Sicilian Vespers). Nelli noted that the murder of Colorado underworld chief Pete Carlino occurred at nearly the same moment as the Luciano-ordered assassination of reigning mafia boss Salvatore Maranzano almost 1,800 miles away in New York City. That these two gangland leaders would be murdered on the same date—a date long associated with a legendary mafia bloodletting—seemed more than coincidence. Through Nelli's research, Colorado boss Carlino was connected, in time of death and occupation but little else, with the most powerful mafia leader of the era.

Three decades later, Betty L. Alt and Sandra K. Wells succeeded in advancing the ball when they published a history of Italian American organized crime in the Rocky Mountain region. Journalist Dick Kreck quickly followed with a history that benefited from recollections of the Smaldone family of Denver.

Author Sam Carlino, descendant of the Pueblo underworld's ruling family, now carries the ball closer than ever to the goal line. Using some circumstantial evidence—reports of Pete Carlino's travels, mention of a little-known but nevertheless significant address in Brooklyn and mutual links to the Danna clan, as well as a forgotten Denver newspaper article—he convincingly builds the connection between Pete Carlino and boss of bosses Maranzano. As he does so, he recounts the significant and often neglected story of the Carlino criminal empire in southern Colorado and Carlino's ill-fated expansion into the Denver region.

Information Age electronic advancement has benefited researchers by providing them with easy access to formerly inaccessible archives. It has also benefited them by providing them with easy access to one another.

Although we live and work on opposite sides of the continental United States, technology permitted me to "meet" Sam Carlino and participate in the final stages of his eight-year effort to bring the Carlino family history to light. It has been my pleasure to become acquainted with Sam, my good fortune to share in his research and my honor to assist him in his important project. While I have tried to bring many neglected crime history stories to the public's attention, I must admit that, until now, I have failed to give Colorado the attention it deserves.

Although Sam has been neither a professional writer nor a historian, his determination to uncover and report this story has molded him into both. And he is well suited to these new roles. He has an innate curiosity, an instinct for identifying the hidden pieces of a puzzle and a resolve to remain with the work until the last pieces are discovered and locked in place. He is an entertaining storyteller, able to weave personal family recollections with historical data to flesh out his subject. In my fairly brief time working with Sam, I have found him to be welcoming and responsive to criticism, eager to explore new angles and generous with his own source materials.

The author's many positive attributes have made his book, *Colorado's Carlino Brothers*, an interesting and useful addition to the organized crime library. The book is certain to secure southern Colorado's mafia its proper place in U.S. underworld history and inspire other researchers to explore additional connections between Colorado and organized crime families across the country.

THOMAS HUNT
Whiting, Vermont
August 2019

Acknowledgements

No book could ever be written without the help and contributions of others to offer a richer experience to the reader. I am so grateful that I was afforded the opportunity to document my grandfather's life in a sincere and accurate format. I would like to recognize my wonderful wife, Adila, and my two remarkable daughters for all of their support throughout this eight-year journey. I juggled time between work, their school obligations and lacrosse games, and I appreciate all three for their support.

I have to thank and acknowledge C.J. Backus for all of her help researching this story as well as proofreading the book. Her never-ending confidence helped me persevere when I would hit a wall of discouragement. C.J. provided me with documents only available from the Denver Public Library that helped form the foundation of the story. C.J. is a lifelong Denver resident and a diligent researcher. Without C.J.'s help, I never would have been able to complete the book.

I want to give special thanks to author and mafia historian Thomas Hunt for writing the foreword to the book. I also want to thank him for all of his sage advice and fact-checking of the Carlino story. He helped me be sure that the book is as accurate as possible. Tom has written several books about the mafia and since 2005 has been the editor and publisher of the mafia-themed newsletter the *Informer*.

A special thanks to Dr. Humbert Nelli for his endorsement of the book. Dr. Nelli was one of the first authors to fact-check the legendary "Night of the Sicilian Vespers" tale that Joe Valachi talked about in *The Valachi*

Papers by Peter Maas. In 1976, Dr. Nelli helped debunk the theory that forty mafia bosses were wiped out in one day on September 10, 1931. He is enjoying retirement after a long career as a professor of history at the University of Kentucky and as an author.

Thanks to Milwaukee mafia historian and author Gavin Schmitt, who unearthed police interviews from 1931 that positively place Pete in Wisconsin meeting with the heads of the Milwaukee mob in late May 1931. His book *The Milwaukee Mafia* is an incredible look at one of the lesser-known mafia strongholds outside New York.

I want to acknowledge *San Jose Mercury News* writer Sal Pizarro for his dedication of keeping San Jose's history alive, as well as informing his readers of the latest events in the Silicon Valley. His dedication to preserving San Jose's past is a throwback to another era, when the beat writers really had a pulse on their community. Sal captures the soul and humanity of the South Bay in his articles.

Thank you to SJSU Professor Emeritus Larry Gerston for his continued advice and support for this project. Larry has authored more than a dozen books and has penned more than one hundred op-ed columns that have been published in the most respected newspapers across the country. His wise advice has helped me prepare myself for what to expect after the book is released. He is a political analyst for KNTV 11 News in San Jose.

Thanks to my friend Michael O'Haire in Long Island, New York, who helped me piece together the Pellegrino Scaglia/Gentile connection and the Paul Danna/Maranzano connection in New York. He is an amazing researcher and diligent fact-checker. I also want to thank him for introducing me to Paul D'Anna. I really enjoyed sharing drinks and stories with him and his brother while visiting Stony Brook, New York. Good luck to him on his upcoming book about his Lopresto family history in Colorado. (It will be a prelude to the Carlino story.)

Special love and thanks to my cousin Susan Carlino Evanoff and her husband, Terry, who provided a plethora of information. Susan provided most of the photos that have never been seen outside the Carlino family. Our long discussions of our grandfather's past have brought us closer and more in tune with the struggle that our fathers had to endure growing up. She provided the group photo of Carlino, Roma, Danna and Cha that deserves to be in a museum.

Special thanks to my cousin Pete Carlino III, who always has a positive word or a funny anecdote to help me continue my quest for the truth about our grandfather's past. Pete III also unearthed six photos of our grandfather's gang while unloading some junk at the dump. Many of those photos are in this book and had never been seen by any of the family before their discovery.

I would like to thank my cousin Steve Carlino for giving me the small trunk that made the arduous trip to California and held the family's most precious items. It means so much to me. I want to thank my friend (and photographer) Michael Soo for the beautiful photographs of the Carlino family trunks that were the catalyst for the downfall of the brothers. My cousin Susan graciously loaned me the big trunk, and Michael captured their significance in an incredible photograph.

Special thanks to my cousin Stacie Carlino Del Giudice, who initiated the scanning of all the old family photos and distributed them to all of the Carlino cousins. Although she was very young, Stacie was present at the San Jose Flea Market when the unknown elderly man informed me of my grandfather's profession and real cause of death while we were working at my sausage stand.

Left: Virginia Carlino, Sam's wife, holding son Sammy Carlino (author), 1967. *Courtesy of the Carlino family collection.*

Right: Sam Carlino, Pete's son, holding son Sammy Carlino (author), 1967. *Courtesy of the Carlino family collection.*

Garden Spot fruit and vegetable stand located in San Jose and operated from 1938 to 1942. Joe and Vic Carlino founded this oasis for weary travelers heading between San Francisco and Los Angeles. All the Carlino boys worked at this roadside business. *Courtesy of the Carlino family collection.*

I would like to thank my Uncle Joe and Uncle Vic for raising my dad and his two brothers during the Depression. Joe and Vic opened the Garden Spot fruit and vegetable stand on Monterey Highway in South San Jose in 1938. All the brothers worked there and learned the grocery business at an early age. One of my dad's responsibilities was making sure the roadside signs had not blown down in the wind. If business was slow, they knew the signs had blown over, and it was his job to run one mile down the road to prop the signs back up. From 1938 to 1942, the Garden Spot was an oasis for weary travelers driving from Los Angeles to San Francisco. Families were refueled with ice-cold orange juice and watermelon.

I would like to thank Paul D'Anna, the grandson of Paul Danna, who allowed me the use of the photograph of his grandfather, John Cha and Jimmy Canzoneri.

Thanks to Artie Crisp at The History Press for taking a chance on me and choosing to publish my manuscript. I had shopped it to about a dozen publishers, and he was the most eager to take on the project. In less than two weeks of shopping the book, I had a deal. He has made the entire process painless.

Most of all, I would like to thank my mom and dad for the wonderful life they provided for me growing up and all of the confidence, support and unconditional love that I try to emulate and bestow on my daughters every day.

Introduction

Throughout my childhood, I was always told my grandfather died of pneumonia. It was not until 1985 that I discovered the truth about my family's past. I was working at our sausage stand at the San Jose Flea Market in California, and while giving samples of Italian sausage to customers, an older man in his mid-seventies sampled a piece. The old-timer took one bite and said he had not tasted Italian sausage that good since Time Market. I then realized he was familiar with our family's Italian sausage recipe, and I told him that it was indeed the Time Market recipe. He immediately asked if I was a Carlino, and as I said yes, he proceeded to tell me how he had known my grandfather, my dad and all of my uncles and how he had worked for my grandfather during Prohibition. This stranger then told me he remembered the day that my grandfather was murdered. "Murdered?" I said. "My grandfather wasn't murdered; he died of pneumonia." The look on his face and the laughter that ensued quickly made me realize that I was about to hear the real story of my grandfather's death.

"Pneumonia," he laughed. "He died of lead poisoning—they shot him up." He informed me that my grandfather was the biggest bootlegger in Colorado during Prohibition and that Pete Carlino and his brother, Sam, controlled almost the entire state. Since our chance meeting over a piece of sausage, I cannot remember his name, nor have I ever met him again.

On my way home that evening, I casually asked my dad, Sam, about his past. First I asked, "What year did you and your brothers come to

California?" He replied, "1932." Then I asked, "When did your mother die?" And he responded, "1935." Then I asked the big one: "How did your father [Pete] die?" He responded the same as he always had and said, "Pneumonia." I loved and respected my dad more than anyone in the world, and I knew if he wasn't telling me the truth it was for a really good reason. I did not press him or even tell him that I knew the truth—there was no need. My cousin who was working with me that day at the sausage stand told everyone in the family about the old man who ran booze for our grandfather. He revealed how the man told us our grandfather was killed in a gruesome fashion. The family secret that had been kept from all of the children was now out. For fifty-five years, the five remaining sons of Pete Carlino had never had a criminal record; they built a successful grocery business and kept their "family's disgrace" a secret. The five Carlino brothers were an important part of their community in San Jose and were loved and revered by many. The disgrace and shame of their family's past was a heavy weight that they had to bear for more than fifty years.

I began my search of my family's history, and the Internet provided a plethora of information, as well as disinformation. Articles about Pete and Sam Carlino began popping up everywhere, and it piqued my interest to find more facts other than what was passed down from my dad and his brothers. In 2009, I read the book *Mountain Mafia* by Betty Alt and Sandra K. Wells. It opened the door to how compelling these events really were. Their book detailed life in my father's family from 1922 to 1932 and filled in many gaps that were not told to me until after 1985. I noticed the numerous newspaper articles that were referenced and began seeking out these same articles to obtain more details. After finding dozens of newspaper clippings, I hit a roadblock. I was speaking on the phone with a librarian at the Denver Public Library, and she suggested I get the help of retired Denver schoolteacher and genealogist C.J. Backus. C.J. located more than two hundred newspaper articles and dozens of photos, as well as traced the Carlino genealogy back to Sicily more than three hundred years.

While researching the history of the mafia in America, I read more than a dozen books, but one stands out: *The Business of Crime: Italians and Syndicate Crime in the United States* by Dr. Humbert Nelli. Dr. Nelli was a professor of history at the University of Kentucky and traveled to more than a dozen mafia-controlled cities across the country to do his research in the early '70s. In 1976, his book documented credible details about the history of the mafia that no other book could match up to that time. He detailed the Salvatore Maranzano murder in New York and even traveled to Denver to research Pete Carlino's murder, which occurred on the same day in 1931. The research he found was astounding but inconclusive regarding whether Pete Carlino had any ties to the New York Mafia. I am proud to say that I found the missing link that verifies that Pete was in New York and met with Maranzano in 1931.

"Fake news" is the new buzzword of this era, and it applies to many of the recent stories I have read about Pete and Sam Carlino. One article I read stated that Pete was shot several times in the head in February 1931 but survived (not true), or that Sam was stabbed to death and his head was cut off and put on a post to send a message to other gangs (not true). Another claim on the Internet was that Pete faked his own death and moved back to Sicily (not true). I wanted to document my father's family's past in a respectful format from reliable sources and give intimate insight into what really happened.

As we approach the one-hundred-year anniversary of Prohibition, "America's greatest social experiment," I find that enough time has passed to document this incredible story—one that's "stranger than a movie thriller," as one headline read in April 1931.

I have had conversations with the offspring of many of the families involved, and I was so relieved to see that they were just like me—searching for the truth and harboring no ill feelings regarding what our families had done to one another almost ninety years ago. I was also encouraged to see the positive response from everyone I knew who had read *Mountain Mafia*. There was a genuine curiosity of the details of our family's past that the book encouraged. I even had a chance to speak to Betty Alt on the phone and had a pleasant conversation about my family's history. (She did, however, misremember a statement I made regarding how I learned about my grandfather's murder. She claimed in a television interview that I didn't know anything until I read her book, but what I *really* said to her was, "I didn't find out until 1985 and was always told he died from pneumonia up 'til then.") As detailed as *Mountain Mafia* was, it focused on a span of ninety years of organized crime in Colorado. This book focuses on Pete and Sam Carlino and the people around them, specifically in the golden age of bootlegging between 1922 and 1932, and dispels many of the erroneous stories that circulate about this period.

Although I am not a writer by trade, I wanted to share the intimate insight I had on my grandfather's past. Numerous characters will be introduced in the beginning; it can become confusing, but they are all relevant participants who play some role within the interlaced fabric of the story. After doing my own extensive research, I realized that there was more to the narrative than has been chronicled. My hope is to share insight and insert a point of view that only a family member can have. The skeletons in my family's closet have been public knowledge in the newspapers since these events occurred, and almost one hundred years have passed since these events took place.

I believe that things happen for a reason, and in hindsight, the death of my grandfather was possibly the "best" thing that could have happened to my dad and his brothers. If those six boys had grown up in that environment long term, I have no doubt that they would have led a life of incarceration or worse. None of Pete Carlino's sons ever had a criminal record. Four of the six brothers served in the military honorably, while my dad, Sam, fought in World War II in the Pacific Theater. My uncle Steve died in a diving accident in Oahu, Hawaii, while assigned on the USS *Enterprise* (CV-6) in June 1941.

My father and his brothers left a legacy that is still intact. In 2018, the Carlino family in San Jose, California, celebrated eighty years of food service in the Santa Clara Valley. Several generations of Carlinos are still involved and continue to keep the Carlino name recognizable—just without the murders and mayhem.

Chapter I

"*24 Ore di Preavviso*"

24 Hours' Notice

Jennie Carlino and her six boys were given twenty-four hours' notice to leave Colorado alive in early October 1932. With her husband, Pete, murdered, her boys were to be raised without a father; everything the family owned was jammed into a 1929 Dodge Senior sedan. She was the mother of six sons ranging in age from four to eighteen years old. Destitute and penniless, the family had been living in squalor in North Denver since the murder of Pete in 1931. Her brother-in-law, Sam Carlino, had met the same fate months before when he was killed in his home by a trusted associate. Jennie held innumerable secrets, and many powerful people in Denver were threatened by what she knew. Jennie's plan was to escape the same fate as the Carlino brothers and disappear into the night, securing a future where her boys would not be raised in constant fear for their lives.

The Carlino boys helped their mother pack the trunk that fit precisely onto the back of their touring sedan. Another smaller trunk was placed inside the vehicle. The Dodge Senior was substandard compared to the Duesenberg they once owned. Jennie chose a handful of cherished items that would make the expedition. The Noritake china set handcrafted from Japan was given a special place in the trunk, as was the Italian crafted wall statue of Saint Therese. There was a rare 1790s violin that Pete bought for his eldest son, Vic, that earned a spot in the trunk. Family photos from happier times, notebooks, ledgers and personal documents also found their

Pete Jr., Sammy, Steve, Jennie, Chuck, Joe and Vic Carlino, 1932. *Courtesy of the Carlino family collection.*

way in. Jennie could not drive, so her two sons Victor and Joe would take turns as pilot and navigator of the steel behemoth that had a ten-foot wheel base and wheels almost three feet high.

The reversal of fortunes throughout Jennie's life must have been disheartening to her as she recollected the meager childhood she once had as a shop owner's daughter, compared to a liquor kingpin's wife

Trunk, statue of St. Therese and violin that made the arduous trip from Denver to San Jose, California, in 1932. *Courtesy of the Sam Carlino family.*

living in a palatial home with a maid. Traveling on a bankroll of funds collected from friends and neighbors, the seven refugees began their flight from Denver.

The brothers navigated the Dodge, heading southwest on Route 66 into Arizona toward their destination of San Diego, California. Jennie's sister-in-law, Josie, had escaped with her children there a year earlier to be close to her father, Philip Piscopo, after her husband, Sam Carlino, was killed in 1931. The two teenage drivers took a wrong right turn while navigating the pine-studded hills south of Flagstaff. Unbeknownst to the brothers, they would be trapped on a narrow one-lane road that traversed the red rock canyon walls of Arizona. Eight-year-old Sammy Carlino was terrified as the extra-large sedan negotiated the tight turns. At times the road was so narrow around the corners that one of the four wheels would be hanging off the cliff as the young boy looked down from an open window into the abyss of the canyon. When an approaching vehicle would be traveling uphill, it was the responsibility of the brothers to back the touring sedan up the hill until a suitable area would appear to allow the car to safely pass. Sam recalled that they were lost on Snebly Road in the Grand Canyon, but after researching the road's name, it was determined to be Schnebly Hill Road, and the brilliant red rock canyons that the eight-year-old boy saw were actually in Sedona, Arizona.

It was serendipitous that the family would arrive in San Diego on Columbus Day 1932. What must have seemed like arriving in a "new land" that Monday brought much hopefulness and promise to a family that had lost everything. In the exuberant dash to greet his cousins and his aunt Josie, eldest son Victor bumped his head on Josie's door jamb so hard it nearly knocked him out. Pete and Sam Carlino's families were reunited once again, and the misfortunes both had endured were now behind them. Jennie and her sons would have a short layover in San Diego before traveling to their final destination of San Jose, California. The drive to San Jose must have felt like a pleasant sojourn compared to the grueling, unpredictable trip they just endured from Denver. Jennie Carlino's parents owned a grocery store in San Jose, and most of her siblings had settled there as well. The brief moments of joy were fleeting, as Jennie would die in 1935 of stomach cancer and leave the two eldest brothers to raise the three youngest boys in the worst depression the country had ever experienced.

Author's Perspective

The most vivid memory my dad had of his life in Colorado was the escape to California in their 1929 Dodge Senior sedan. He told me the story countless times, and I was always intrigued by the road they had taken. As an eight-year-old boy, he thought they were in the Grand Canyon. I had hiked to the bottom of the Grand Canyon three times, and I knew that no such road existed. Just before he died, we searched the primitive Internet on my laptop, and I was unable to find the infamous Snebly Road that was ingrained in this terrified boy's memories. In November 2002, just two months after my dad's passing, I was in Sedona, Arizona, and stumbled on a primitive 4x4 road that traverses the red rock canyons traveling east to west. It connected Arizona State Highway 17 to Sedona, and it is named Schnebly Hill Road; it is generally only traveled by vehicles with four-wheel-drive.

When I bought my Ford Expedition in Colorado, I drove back to California via Schnebly Hill Road and was able to experience what my dad had always described to me. I was in awe of its beauty, and I tried to put myself in this young boy's position. It was really hard to experience what he endured because I had four-wheel-drive, snow tires, air conditioning, power steering, power brakes, GPS and a cellphone. I actually knew where I was going, and the narrow one-lane road has been widened since the 1930s.

Chapter 2

"Tutto in Famiglia"

ALL IN THE FAMILY

The Carlinos originated from the town of Lucca Sicula in the Agrigento region of Sicily. Lucca has a mountainous terrain and a dry, arid climate. Lemon, orange and olive trees grace the rugged terrain of this ancient island. Repression from the corrupt Sicilian government prompted thousands to flee the region in the late 1800s, and many headed to America. On October 17, 1888, Vito Carlino, Pete and Sam's father, arrived in New Orleans, Louisiana, with his friends Calogero Parlapiano, Guiseppe Mortillaro and Vito Colletti (brother of Guiseppe Mortillaro's wife, Vincenza). Mortillaro would soon change his name to Riggio. Guiseppe Riggio would stay and raise a family in their new country, but Vito Carlino would return to Sicily after only one year in America. Waiting back in Sicily, he had a five-year-old boy, Stefano (Steve), and a newborn, Pietro Antonio (Pete).

Vito would eventually make plans to have his entire family move to the United States. By 1897, he had added two more children to his family: Salvatore (Sam), seven years old, and Mariantonia (Mary), nine months. On October 11, 1897, his wife, Calogera (Carrie), and their children sailed on the French ship *Chateau Yquem*, departing from Palermo, Sicily, and arriving in New Orleans.[1] Vito would arrive two weeks later from Palermo on the ship *Montebello*. In 1898, fifteen-year-old Stefano would arrive in New Orleans from Palermo. Vito Carlino moved his family to Southern Colorado, following their friends the Riggio family to Vineland, to the rich soils of the St. Charles Mesa. They began their new life as farmers. In 1900,

Calogera (Carrie) Carlino, Stefano Carlino (five years old) and baby Pietro Antonio (Pete) Carlino (one and a half years old), Lucca Sicula, Sicily, 1888. *Courtesy of the Carlino family collection.*

Carlo (Charlie) was born. Mary was the only daughter born to Vito and Carrie. There is no record of her death, but it is assumed that she died young, before 1910.

Lucca Sicula is a small town in Sicily about forty miles south of Palermo. Pueblo, Colorado, is the sister city of Lucca Sicula. Many families fled the oppression of Sicily and started a new life in the "land of opportunity." Just after 1900, there was a boom of immigrants arriving not just from Sicily, but from all of Italy. Once word got back to Lucca Sicula how fertile the land was and how Pueblo had rich mining and steel production, the rush was on. The Carlino, Riggio, D'Anna, Colletti, Mulé, Parlapiano, Piscopo, Giarratano, Maniscalco, La Rocca, Vaccaro and Mortillaro families originated from this small town known for its olive oil and orange trees.[2]

The Carlino family were working their farmland on their Vineland Ranch, where they grew sugar beets. On November 5, 1912, Carlino patriarch Vito

Vincenza Ferraro Carlino and Stefano Carlino. *Courtesy of the Carlino family collection.*

Carlino died at the age of fifty-nine.[3] Vito suffered from bronchial asthma. He was buried at Roselawn Cemetery in Pueblo.

Vito's eldest son, Steve, married Vincenza (Anna) Ferraro on October 23, 1904, in Pueblo. Steve was a real estate and loan agent, sold insurance and was a notary public. He worked for the Carroll-Vreeland Real Estate Company. He resided at 1005 East Abriendo Avenue in Pueblo. "Steve was the brains of the outfit," recalled Pete's son Sam. Steve applied for a petition of naturalization in 1910 and attained U.S. citizenship in 1914. He did not embrace the farmer's lifestyle, as the city of Pueblo suited his intellectual skills better. By 1918, Steve and his wife had moved to Manhattan, New York. Five months after moving to Manhattan, Steve Carlino was found murdered around 7:00 a.m. on August 27, 1918.[4] He had sustained gunshot wounds to the right lung, stomach, liver and small vertebrae. His official cause of death was listed as a homicide, and his killer was never found.

Pete was the second-oldest son of Vito Carlino. Standing five-foot-six, he did not have an imposing physical appearance, but he made up for it in tenacity and hubris. His drooping right eye was a genetic trait that was passed down through generations of many Sicilians, as several of

Left: Salvatore (Sam) Carlino. *Courtesy of the Carlino family collection.*

Right: Jennie Riggio Carlino. *Courtesy of the Carlino family collection.*

his sons would have the same feature. Pete's early childhood was spent in Sicily until arriving in America at age ten. His English was spoken with an obvious, thick Sicilian dialect, unlike his brother Sam, who had learned to speak English at an earlier age. Sam was the more dapper and debonair of the two brothers and was always impeccably dressed. The brothers had little schooling once they arrived in the new country, but both learned to read and write English.

The Carlinos and Riggios moved from Louisiana to Colorado in 1898. The two families were close, and Pete fell in love with Guiseppe Riggio's second-oldest daughter, Giovana (Jennie). Pete Carlino married Jennie Riggio on June 14, 1913. She was born in Louisiana in 1894, one of many children Guiseppe and Vincenza would bear in America. In June 1914, Pete and Jennie had their first child, Vito (Vic), and by 1916, their second son, Guiseppe (Joe), had arrived.

Unbeknownst to the Carlino brothers, the State of Colorado was about to change their lives forever. Colorado legislators enacted their own form of prohibition on January 1, 1916, four years before the entire nation would go dry in 1920. Colorado outlawed the production and sale of all intoxicating beverages with the exception of use for religious or medicinal purposes.[5] This gave Colorado a four-year head start on bootlegging. Soon those fields of sugar beets on the Carlino farm would be turned into "Sugar Moon" and sold as distilled moonshine to local miners and ironworkers. Their poor management of money precipitated a new vocation. The brothers Pete and Sam Carlino were struggling as farmers, and in 1917, they would lose their farm to foreclosure and move to Sugar City. The brothers continued to farm sugar beets on their new smaller plot of land and continued to make bootleg whiskey. In 1917, Pete's younger brother, Charlie, was working for the Colorado Steelworks.

Pietro Antonio (Pete) Carlino. *Courtesy of the Carlino family collection.*

The D'Anna (Danna) brothers— John, Vito, Tony and Sam—emigrated from Lucca Sicula to Pueblo starting in 1898 and knew the Carlinos and Mortillaros from their village in Sicily. Seventeen-year-old Giovanni (John) Danna arrived on October 3, 1898,[6] and moved to Pueblo. By 1904, John had attained American citizenship. Sixteen-year-old Vito (Pete) Danna arrived on September 6, 1906, on the ship *Roma*.[7] He departed Naples and arrived in New York. Twenty-two-year-old Antonio

Vito (Vic) and Giuseppe (Joe) Carlino, Pete and Jennie's sons, 1917. *Courtesy of the Carlino family collection.*

(Tony) Danna arrived six weeks later on October 24, 1906. Tony also arrived on the ship *Roma*.[8] Standing five-foot-eight, Tony had brown hair and brown eyes and had a mark on his temple. The last of the four Danna brothers was seventeen-year-old Salvatore (Sam) Danna, who arrived in 1911. The Dannas were living in Vineland, Colorado, as farmers, and the Carlinos owned a farm adjacent to the Danna property. The Dannas were making moonshine on their farm, and a rivalry was renewed.

A rumor stated that the two families had some conflict dating back to their time in Sicily. Sicilians historically are hard-pressed to forget a disagreement. The concept of the *vendetta* is ingrained into the Sicilian culture dating back hundreds of years. Pride and honor are at the root of a vendetta, and disputes are rarely settled without bloodshed. It is a unique cultural ritual that is difficult to comprehend if one is not accustomed to it.

Philip Piscopo's daughters would eventually make the Carlino and the Danna family related as brothers-in-law. Pete Danna would marry Philip's daughter Anna Piscopo on January 18, 1913. Three years later, Philip's younger daughter, Josephine (Josie), would marry Sam Carlino in Pueblo, Colorado. The Carlinos and the Dannas were now family. Joe Piscopo was a friend of John Danna, and his sister Mary Piscopo married John on July 18, 1902. Joe and Mary Piscopo were siblings and were cousins to Anna and Josephine Piscopo. When Sam Carlino married Josephine Piscopo, it bonded the Carlinos and Dannas by matrimony but opened a wound that had been festering since the two families' tenure in Sicily. The root of the vendetta is unclear, but having the Carlinos and Dannas related by marriage did not help their situation. For Sicilians, being family by marriage did not carry the same significance as being family by blood.

AUTHOR'S PERSPECTIVE

Guiseppe Mortillaro changed his named to Riggio to escape his past in Sicily. My dad had told me that he was a "really mean tough old guy." The climate toward Southern Italians (especially Sicilians) in New Orleans was quite contentious at that time. In 1891, eleven Sicilians were lynched in retribution for Police Chief Hennessy's murder. My dad said that New Orleans was too volatile for Grandpa Riggio, so he moved to Southern Colorado. The town of Lucca Sicula is very small and close-knit, and it is not surprising that so many of its inhabitants ended up in Pueblo, Colorado.

Steve Carlino was rumored to have been a mob accountant in New York. Maybe this was the reason for his murder.

Chapter 3

"La Nascita della Criminalità Organizzata"

THE BIRTH OF ORGANIZED CRIME

L ike in Pueblo, Little Italys began springing up across the country. The Sicilian peasant community in Pueblo solidified and occupied regions east of town. Local Pueblo residents resented their new neighbors to the east, and the Italian community as a whole endured an onslaught of racism and xenophobia.

The "Black Hand" was a term nativist Coloradans used to describe most Italians in this era, whether they committed unlawful acts or not. The term was coined as early as 1903 to describe mafia activities, especially when applied for extortion. Anonymous letters would be mailed or delivered to mostly Sicilian immigrants who were suspected of having a lot of cash. Many families' life savings were extorted through threats of violence from the Black Handers if they did not pay up. An imprint of a small hand in black ink was the signature for many of the letters. By 1908, newspaper writers were using the name "Black Hand" as a substitute for "mafia." Recently arriving immigrants were easy targets because of their distrust of the police, as the Black Handers counted on their silence. Occasionally, police reports would be filed, and the culprits would be caught. Arrest reports noted that every Black Hand case involved a victim living in a section of town composed of a large proportion of immigrants. In 1915, Black Hand letters began to decrease once prosecutors used federal mail fraud laws to catch their prey.[9] By making it a federal offense to defraud by mail, it was more likely that the ones hand-delivering the letters could be identified. By 1916, Colorado legislators were unknowingly creating a new scheme for the Black Handers to make money. Prohibition was coming to Colorado, and many of the Black Handers became bootleggers.

The criminalization of alcoholic beverages was being touted by the Protestant hardliners, as the Catholic community lobbied hard against the Peterson Prohibition Statute, to no avail.[10] Wine was an important ingredient to the fabric of many Italian families' daily lives. It was food, it fostered kinship and it helped sustain fellowship. To many Italian and Sicilian families, wine was consumed on a daily basis, and it made no sense to outlaw something so sacred to their culture and well-being.

Carrie Nation helped kickstart the temperance movement that led many women's groups to pick up axes and break up popular bars and saloons.[11] Standing six feet tall, Carrie Nation was an intimidating force, especially when wielding her axe. Although she would not live to see it, Carrie Nation helped turn the tide of public opinion, with the help of the Protestant community and even the local Ku Klux Klan, for outlawing alcohol, inadvertently helping to create organized crime as we know it today. Xenophobia toward immigrants and their culture (especially Italian Catholics) drove the support of the KKK. Colorado has a dark history of KKK activity, and the group's influence peaked during the mid-1920s.[12]

Carrie A. Nation helped kickstart the temperance movement. *Courtesy of Wikimedia Commons.*

Flood damage in downtown Pueblo, 1921. *Courtesy of the Carlino family collection.*

Overnight there was an immediate demand for alcoholic beverages that the public craved, and those who supplied the need were instantly made criminals. By 1917, Pete and Sam Carlino had begun distilling "Sugar Moon," a homemade moonshine made from sugar beets. The brothers had moonshine stills hidden around the countryside and inside caves built into the landscape. With Colorado passing its "Bone Dry Act," it turned honest farmers into outlaws and family neighbors into bootleg rivals.

By 1920, the Carlino brothers had moved to Crowley County, Colorado. Pete and Jennie Carlino added two more boys to their family, Carlo (Chuck) and Stefano (Steve).[13] Sam Carlino and his family lived on the same ranch property with his brother Pete. Sam and Josephine had one boy and a girl at the time. Pete and Sam's younger brother, Charlie, married Carrie Barbera and lived on a farm with his mother, Calogera (Carrie). Unbeknownst to the brothers, the next decade would be one of bloodshed and strife.

On the evening of June 3, 1921, the Arkansas River in Pueblo crested and the levee broke, allowing an ocean of water to engulf the town.[14] Although warning sirens had been sounded, the residents mostly ignored the alarms

Pueblo flood damage along the Arkansas River. *Courtesy of the Carlino family collection.*

because they had survived smaller storms in the past and felt this would be more of the same. When the torrent of water had subsided, the level of devastation became apparent. Nearly 650 homes and businesses had been destroyed, and the death toll neared one hundred.

Seven thousand people were homeless in Pueblo. "The flood of 1921 was the single most important event in the history of Pueblo," stated Joanne West Dodd, a local historian. Pueblo's downtown was in ruins, and it was prime pickings for unsavory businessmen to exploit. World War I had ended, and the short-lived prosperity that is synonymous with the building of a war machine ended too. The effects on the economy were still taking a toll, especially in flood-torn Pueblo. Industrial layoffs had spun the city into a stupor. Since the passing of the Volstead Act in 1920, the federal government had outlawed the production and distribution of any intoxicating beverages in all forty-eight states. Colorado had a four-year head start on most of the country and had the networks in place to fill the need for what the public desired most: a drink.

AUTHOR'S PERSPECTIVE

The introduction of Prohibition was the single biggest factor that caused the mafia to grow so quickly. Across the United States, there were regional groups of mafia families tied to their roots from their hometown regions in Sicily. Without Prohibition, those groups would not have grown to the size achieved by the 1950s.

The KKK had more influence in Colorado from 1900 to 1930 than most people realized. Phil Goodstein wrote a wonderful book titled *In the Shadow of the Klan: When the KKK Ruled Denver, 1920–1926*. It dives deep into Colorado's dark past of racism and xenophobia and how the group controlled government and police agencies at the highest levels in Colorado. The KKK's role in passing dry laws cannot be overlooked.

Chapter 4

"Lasciato per Morto"

LEFT FOR DEAD

Pellegrino Scaglia (aka Tony Viola) was a local merchant and bootlegger who distributed Carlino booze in Pueblo, but he had a much larger role in the organized crime syndicate in Pueblo than most are aware of. Scaglia changed his named to Antonio Viola around 1916, although he used his real name on his registration for the war on September 12, 1918.

Scaglia arrived in New York in 1905 at the age of twenty-two. His trip was paid for by his cousin Salvatore Valenti (his mother was Anna Marie Valenti). He was arrested in St. Louis in 1911 for the murder of Bartholdi Cardinali in New York City. Scaglia and Cardinali's family had played together as children back in their home town of Burgio in the Agrigento province of Sicily, very close to Lucca Sicula.[15]

In 1908, the Cardinali brothers—Giuseppe, Bartholdi and Vincenzo—accused Scaglia of writing Black Hand letters to their friends and confronted him at their benevolent society meeting. An argument ensued, and Giuseppe slapped Scaglia in the face (a grievous insult to a Sicilian) in front of a crowd. One day later, Giuseppe Cardinali's lifeless body was found in Coffey Park, New York, with bullet holes and stab wounds. Pellegrino Scaglia fled to St. Louis and was living there for more than a year before the Cardinalis tracked him down. One evening in 1909 on Dago Hill in St. Louis, Pellegrino Scaglia was stabbed by three men more than forty-three times and left for dead. Scaglia miraculously survived but was severely disfigured.[16] A vendetta had been set in motion, and after a time of recuperation, Scaglia returned to New York to exact his revenge.

Pellegrino Scaglia (aka Tony Viola). *From the* St. Louis Star and Times, *August 5, 1911.*

Joe Carlino's baptism certificate. Pellegrino Scaglia's wife, Maria, was godmother, 1916. *Courtesy of the Carlino family collection.*

On July 29, 1911, New York barber Bartholdi Cardinali was killed instantly from a shotgun blast while sitting in his window sill at 344 East Twenty-First Street in New York City.

Scaglia was indicted for the murder and was extradited from St. Louis to New York by two New York City police officers. Bartholdi's brother Vincenzo Cardinali accompanied the officers to identify Scaglia before the arrest. Judge Grimm of Missouri noted, "It is better to surrender to another state a man who may seem to be innocent and let him prove his innocence there, than to weaken the comity between the states and to risk making the state an asylum for criminals….If this prisoner is innocent he will be able to prove that fact in New York. I am not unmindful that for that in case he is innocent this extradition will work a hardship on him but it is better to risk inflicting such a hardship than to do anything which may aid the escaped of the guilty from punishment."[17] In 1912, Scaglia beat the murder charge and headed west.

Pellegrino Scaglia married Maria Occomando on November 21, 1914, in Pueblo. By 1916, Scaglia had changed his name to Tony Viola and owned a grocery store with partner Joe Cusomano (who would marry John Mulay's daughter Carrie) at 902 Elm Street in Pueblo.[18] Scaglia was a friend to the Carlinos, and his wife, Maria (Scaglia), became godmother to baby Joe Carlino (Pete Carlino's second-oldest son).

The Scaglias would have three children: Philip, Anna Marie and baby Rosie (Penny). Scaglia was distributing the Carlino brothers' liquor through his grocery store on Elm Street.

His store was in direct competition with Frank Bacino's soft drink parlor, which was the main outlet for the Danna brothers' booze.

Pellegrino Scaglia lived adjacent to his grocery store at 904 Elm Street. His son Philip and daughter Anna Marie were playmates of Frank Cordaro, who lived next door with his parents at 906 Elm Street.[19] Frank Cordaro's father, Vito, worked for the Colorado Fuel and Iron Company.[20] The family had lived in New York before moving to Pueblo. Vito was an artificial flower maker back in New York City. He was married to Emmanuela Maniscalco. Emmanuela was most likely a cousin of Pete and Sam Carlino's. The Carlino brothers' grandmother was named Mariantonia Maniscalco. By 1918, Scaglia was operating a pool hall in Pueblo on Elm Street in addition to his grocery store.[21]

On May 6, 1922, around 11:00 a.m., Pellegrino Scaglia; his four-year-old daughter, Anna Marie; and nine-year-old Frank Cordaro were riding in his horse-pulled grocery wagon when they were atttacked.[22] The three were traveling west on East Mesa Avenue directly in front of the gate at St. Mary's Church and School.[23] A sedan slowed beside them, and shotgun blasts tore through Scaglia and the Cordaro boy. Scaglia fell on top of his daughter Anna Marie to protect her from the blasts. Young Cordaro was thrown from the wagon, and his head was crushed by the rear wheel. It was later determined that he was riddled with buckshot and probably died before being crushed by the cart. Anna Marie was found alive and unharmed but covered in her father's blood and severely traumatized. Bystander John Zbanosick was caught in the crossfire and received nonthreatening wounds from the shotgun blasts.

After the attack, a dragnet was issued in the surrounding counties. Pueblo police were unable to identify the shooters, but the Dodge touring car with Colorado plate no. 21-066 had been reported stolen. Scaglia had a loaded revolver hidden under the seat of his cart but never had a chance to defend himself. It was reported that Scaglia was the Black Hand leader of Pueblo and approached the Dannas, attempting to befriend them to some extent and "tone down" the animosity that had sprung up between the two families.[24] Scaglia's death was so significant that it warranted a meeting of the U.S. mafia heads to settle.

Scaglia's murder was an unsanctioned hit on someone who is now believed to have been the head of the Pueblo mafia in 1922. According to Nicola Gentile, the murder of Scaglia caused a split in the Colorado family (Danna/Carlino). Gentile was the *capo* (head) of the Kansas City faction and was the mediator for the mafia trial. Gentile wrote a book, *Vita di Capomafia*

(*Life of a Mafia Leader*), published in 1963, after he was deported back to Sicily. Gentile was born in the town of Siciliana in the Agrigento region of Sicily, about forty-five kilometers from Lucca Sicula. It is the most significant and informative description of life in the *Onorata Società* (Honored Society), aka La Cosa Nostra, that had been published up to that date. Books by Joe Valachi and Joe Bonanno would have other significant descriptions of the early days of the mafia but would be published years later.

Nicola Gentile stated the following in his book about the murder of Pellegrino Scaglia in Pueblo:[25]

> *This is how it happened:*
>
> *One of the brothers, Pellegrino Scaglia was killed following a noisy argument which brought a split in the family of Pueblo, Colorado. In the struggle many young men fell. The younger brother, the father-in-law and a nephew of the victim transferred themselves to Kansas City. In the meantime they were called to New York to appear before the General Assembly to respond to the grave accusations formulated by Mr. La Rocca.*
>
> *As it has always been shown, since the beginning the General Assembly which functioned in truth like a Court of Assize, was composed of elements who were nearly all illiterate. The eloquence was that which impressed the ears, and the more one knew how to speak the more they heeded and it ended by your will being imposed on that mass of boors.*
>
> *The accuser, LaRocca, who had caused the assembly to convene began to enumerate all the misdeeds of the three above named and many things that did not correspond to the truth were said with cunning.*
>
> *After the enumeration of the charges against the accused which included me, the representatives return to the council room to express the verdict.*
>
> *Meanwhile Toto D'Aquila, as capo dei capi (head of heads) gave the leading address and summarized all the developments of the dispute and, therefore, giving his recommendation for the condemnation to death of the three above-mentioned. The other representatives in order of succession, join the verdict of Toto D'Aquila. No sooner, however, was it my turn to give my opinion than I asked to be allowed to ask another question of the accuser, and conceding me that authority, I had him called, to when I addressed a point-blank question. He did not know how to respond in a clear manner and precisely for which, he left all in doubt. Not being able to give their judgment serenely, it was necessary to adjourn the debate which was postponed and it was scheduled to be held at Pittsburgh fifteen days later.*

On the fix date, Toto D'Aquila, who functioned as President of the Tribunal, not being able to preside at that session sent his substitute Giuseppe Traina, nicknamed "Lu Viddanu" (the peasant).

No sooner had Traina arrived at Pittsburgh, than he approached me and requested me in order to be able to bring to an end the case which already had been dragged on about two years, to abandon the tenacious defense of the three for whom already there had been the pronouncement of sentence to death. He made me understand moreover and also in an explicit fashion that if I did not abandon my position to defend them to the bitter end, it could be that the same thing would befall me. Scornful of the danger with which I was faced and at the same time, more convinced than ever of the innocence of the three, I try to make them understand my point of view, upon which I based the defense. It was not possible, in fact, I asserted, that the three accused could have, in order to avenge themselves for the death of their dear one, to shoot those of the opposing party of Pueblo, Colorado and immediately cross the frontier to Kansas City, because between the first city and the second runs a distance of about 600 miles. It would have been possible if the events had happened between New York and Brooklyn, cities which are joined by a bridge. Furthermore, there was another reason to believe in the innocence of the three accused that pushed me to demand the acquittal of the three. It was based on the fact that in the shelter of Kansas City, territory of my jurisdiction, I could instigate a recall for arbitration and therefore, of insubordination, which I had been made to understand in the assembly. Finally the substitute (Traina) convinced that what I asserted was in keeping with the truth, called the accuser from him he wanted to know if he had the intention to put an end to the dispute. Having a clear refusal, he left him to his destiny, meanwhile acquitting the three, making it clear that in view of what had happened at Pueblo, Colorado, the three were expelled as they were from the Family of Kansas City.

Like this was closed the grievous case that was dragged out for about two years.

This excerpt from Gentile's book demonstrates how swift Sicilian justice can be imparted by the judge, jury and executioner of the mafia's legal system. After a disagreement, a man named LaRocca opposed Pellegrino's brother Mariano Scaglia; father-in-law, Frank Accomondo; and nephew Luca Colletti. Evidently, the three transferred to Kansas City, Missouri, to avoid the bloodshed occurring in Colorado and were accused of an unwarranted response to the Scaglia murder. The three were disputed by La Rocca. The general assembly was leaning in favor of a guilty verdict of the Scaglia *compari* until Gentile stepped in and cross-examined LaRocca. Gentile, realizing that he could face the same fate as the defendants, swayed the general assembly that La Rocca's testimony was false. The accuser, LaRocca, was given a chance to put an end to the dispute but declined in the hope of a guilty verdict. It was determined that LaRocca had exaggerated his claims and, according to the assembly, would "be left to his destiny."

According to Federal Bureau of Investigation (FBI) interviews of Philip Scaglia, Pellegrino's son, in 1964, the "LaRocca" whom Nicola Gentile was speaking of in his book was most likely Frank LaRocca.[26] The FBI was tracking down all leads from Gentile's statements in his book, and the details of an obscure bootlegger killed in Pueblo, Colorado, while delivering groceries in a horse-pulled wagon forty years earlier seemed pertinent. When asked by the FBI how his father, Pellegrino Scaglia, was killed, Philip responded that "he had always been told his Dad died of pneumonia." Apparently, "pneumonia" must be a Sicilian code for "killed by shotgun."

Frank LaRocca was born in Lucca Sicula, Sicily, in February 1889. He arrived in America on October 24, 1906, and was traveling under the name Francesco Franco. He was arrested in Kansas City, Missouri, two times for murder. In 1920, he was acquitted by a jury, and in 1921, he was a suspect but released.[27] Frank LaRocca died on December 27, 1976.

Nicola Gentile's life in the *Onorata Società* was so extraordinary that he has been called the "Forrest Gump of the Mafia." His book details numerous events in so many different cities that some mafia historians discredit some of his stories.[28] Many doubt that he was as close to so many pivotal events as he claimed. The fact that Gentile was living in Sicily in the 1960s when he published his book is most interesting. He described an event in Pueblo, Colorado, in 1922 involving Pellegrino Scaglia with such detail that it truly rings of the truth. Why would Gentile recall the murder of an obscure bootlegger delivering groceries in a horse-pulled wagon more than forty years before if the story weren't true? Gentile most likely embellished some of the details while recounting many of his stories, but the basis of the Scaglia ordeal seems legitimate. Gentile mentioned in his book that in 1915 he and his brother visited Pueblo and were offered much warmth and treated to many feasts by his friend Vincenzo Chiappetta, who was a cousin to Pellegrino Scaglia.[29]

After the death of Pellegrino Scaglia, the Carlino brothers assumed his position as liquor lords of Pueblo, and as Nicola Gentile stated in his book, "In the struggle many young men fell." The Carlino brothers were about to be challenged for their stake in the Southern Colorado bootlegging market.

AUTHOR'S PERSPECTIVE

The connection between Pellegrino Scaglia and the Carlinos is one of the most important links established in this book. Scaglia's relatives were put on trial (a mafia trial), and their lives depended on Nicola Gentile's cross-examination of LaRocca. Gentile's involvement and recollection of this incident shed light on how these families operated in the early 1920s. After Scaglia was murdered, the Carlino brothers and Danna brothers went to war over who will control Southern Colorado's bootleg territories.

I want to thank my friend Michael O'Haire, who shared the Gentile book *Vita di Capomafia*, as well as recently released FBI files. Valuable information about Scaglia was released in the latest document dump from the JFK murder investigation. I still find it puzzling that the FBI would track down the son of a bootlegger whose father was killed forty years before Kennedy was assassinated.

Chapter 5

"*Gli Associati*"

THE ASSOCIATES

By 1923, Pete Carlino's family had moved to Model, Colorado. Pete and Jennie had added a baby girl to the family. Carrie Carlino was born on November 19, 1922, but only lived to be three years old. Her older brothers adored her and played with her often. Eldest brother Vic suffered a serious eye injury when the three-year-old accidentally poked him in the eye with an umbrella. Vic would lose his sight from that eye but kept it a secret for most of his life. Carrie suffered a painful death as a child when she was inflicted with "acute yellow atrophy of the liver." Her nine-year-old brother, Joe, ran into town to summon a doctor, but it was too late. Carrie died on December 7, 1925. Unfortunately, Pete and Jennie would suffer the loss of a daughter just as his parents had endured more than twenty years before. Carrie would be the only girl Pete and Jennie would ever have.

Frank Bacino was a friend of the Danna family and a well-known figure in the Italian community in Pueblo. Bacino had immigrated to the United States in 1890. He had a colorful existence once he arrived in Pueblo. On February 10, 1903, Bacino was shot three times. Police found him lying on his back with two wounds in one leg and one in another.[30] The officers asked who shot him, but he refused to tell them any details of the incident. He stated that he didn't have an enemy on Earth. The police believed he was lying and suspected jealousy on the part of another Italian man for a woman with whom Bacino had been rather friendly. Bacino even refused to go to the hospital and went directly home after the incident.

The only known photo of Carrie Carlino, taken in 1925. *Courtesy of the Carlino family collection.*

Nine years later, in June 1912, Bacino was arrested for the padding of payrolls while working at a commissary car for the Missouri Pacific Railroad.[31] Special agents arrested Bacino, and he was placed under a bond by the justice of the peace until the case could be tried. On February 28, 1915, Bacino was shot again at his store at 119 West First Street in Pueblo.[32] Bacino and Bernardo Maniscalco (Pete Carlino's cousin) were shot by four men. Bacino and Maniscalco returned fire with their own handguns, and both men fell to the ground wounded. (Tony Marino, Alfonso Cardinale, Samuel Galando and Tony Galando were arrested after leaving a doctor's office for treatment of the wounds they received during the shooting.) More than forty-five shots were fired during the melee.

Frank Bacino was the uncle of Rosa (Rose), Joe Piscopo's wife. Frank opened the Bacino Brothers Grocery on Santa Fe Avenue in Pueblo with his two brothers, Calogero and Charles.[33] The flood of 1921 did not spare the brothers' store, and they were forced to vacate their location on Santa Fe Avenue. After the flood, Frank Bacino opened a soft drink parlor near Union Avenue in Pueblo.[34] The parlor was merely a front for bootleg whiskey being produced by the Danna brothers. The Dannas had a network of stills in caves and shanties around the St. Charles Mesa area, as well as two whiskey stills on their farm in Vineland.

John Mulé (pronounced "Mulay" and later changed to this phonetic spelling) was a family friend of the Riggios and Carlinos. John's brother Calogero (Carl) Mulay was married to Catherine Riggio. Catherine Mulay and Jennie Carlino were sisters, which made Pete Carlino and Carl Mulay brothers-in-law. In 1923, John Mulay opened the American Pool Hall at 224 Union Avenue in Pueblo, located just blocks from Frank Bacino's soft drink parlor.[35] Since the death of Pellegrino Scaglia, the pool hall had become the main distribution outlet for the Carlinos' brand of bootlegged beverages and, in the process, the closest rival to the Dannas' outlet of bootleg shine. The proximity of the two distribution sites created more unneeded animosity between the Carlinos and Dannas.

The Dannas and Carlinos were not only a feuding family but also rival bootleggers jockeying for position in Southern Colorado's lucrative moonshine business. Pueblo's two major bootlegging factions were about to galvanize the families down a path of blood for the next seven years. Vendettas would stain their relationship, and blood would stain the streets of Pueblo.

The Dannas allegedly drew first blood with the murder of Pellegrino Scaglia. John Mulay was next. On February 27, 1923, just after about 11:00 p.m., Mulay was closing up his pool hall on Union Avenue with his son, John Jr.[36] John Sr. and his son rode a streetcar to the corner of Mesa and Evans to retrieve his touring car, which was parked only a few blocks from his house. Mulay was slaughtered with a technique we now refer to as a "drive-by." As he was opening the door of his car, an approaching sedan slowed down with curtains drawn, and suddenly a blast from a short-barreled shotgun tore into his chest. John Mulay's son ducked for cover and was only able to ascertain that the car had window curtains and no license plates. Witnesses stated that Mulay's son knelt beside the

John Mulay Jr.,
January 14, 1929.
*Courtesy of the Carlino
family collection.*

body and offered a quiet prayer before he could be heard swearing an oath of vengeance. If John Jr. saw who killed his father, he would never have disclosed it to the police. To a Sicilian, revenging a murder is the most notorious manifestation of the vendetta.

Carl Mulay would be the Dannas' next target for assassination. After the killing of his brother John, Carl Mulay asked the Carlinos to help protect him with a bodyguard from Denver named Vincenzo Urso.[37] Urso was Carl's companion for the next four months, and both men carried concealed handguns; Urso's was a Smith & Wesson .38 special. Carl's premonition of an attempt on his life became a reality. On the evening of June 19, 1923, Mulay and Urso were parked on Main Street near the American Pool Hall when a sedan slowed beside Mulay's car. Urso took several shotgun blasts to the head and body, while Mulay narrowly escaped. Carl Mulay drove off with trepidation to Santa Fe Avenue near Goat Hill and fled from the car to safety. Pueblo police extracted the Ford, which was riddled with holes from two separate shotgun attacks, and located Carl Mulay later that evening.

Joe Piscopo and his brother-in-law, Jim Giarratano, were arrested a few days later and charged with the murder of Vincenzo Urso and the attempted murder of Carl Mulay. After futile testimony from numerous witnesses, the coroner's jury was forced to release Piscopo and Giarratano. Witnesses were afraid to testify. Whether Piscopo and Giarratano were responsible for the shooting or not, they had both become targets of the Carlinos.[38] Here again a Mulay would not divulge to the Pueblo police the shooters involved and would eventually let swift Sicilian justice be the decisive factor in the vendetta.

AUTHOR'S PERSPECTIVE

The *vendetta* is such a unique phenomenon in Sicilian culture that it is really hard for an educated, twenty-first-century mind to comprehend. Pride and honor are the driving force of this ancient ritual. Once the *vendetta* had begun, it was inevitable that many people would be lost along the way. The silence that John Mulay Jr. and Carl Mulay exhibited after witnessing two separate murders is extraordinary. These men had been steadfast in their belief that retribution would eventually come to the perpetrators by Sicilians and not by law enforcement. I was told that the Mulé family changed their name to Mulay because it was always mispronounced, so it was changed to be spelled phonetically so Americans could pronounce it properly.

Chapter 6

"Calogero"

CHARLIE

I n the summer of 1923, Pete Carlino's youngest brother, Carlo (Charlie), made several trips to the Danna ranch in Vineland. Charlie was the only son of Vito Carlino who had been born in America. He was raised on the farm adjacent to the Danna ranch as a child and knew the family well. Different accounts state that he was either there for a peace offering or for intimidation. One account later cited by John Danna's testimony was that Charlie was trying to get the Dannas to extort money from neighboring farmers. Regardless of his intentions, Charlie was now in the Dannas' crosshairs and would inevitably be the next victim of this conflict.[39]

The feud between the Carlino brothers and the Dannas did not have the same notoriety as the Hatfields and McCoys, but it was a skirmish that would manifest its own infamy that would live to this day in Pueblo. Since 2004, Puebloans gather in October to witness the "Pueblo Ghost Walk" event.[40] Historians reenact events in the streets of Pueblo that had an impact on the area, and the "Baxter Bridge Shootout" is one of the favorites.

On September 10, 1923, the feud between the Carlinos and Dannas escalated at the Baxter Road bridge near the Old Santa Fe Trail where it crossed the Arkansas River east of Pueblo.[41] Witness accounts differ on the details of the shootout. According to some, two cars were approaching each other, passed on the bridge and stopped on opposite ends; the occupants of the cars dispersed and began the firefight. Another account, according to the Danna brothers, noted that Charlie Carlino and another man were waiting to ambush them in a cornfield, where the skirmish ensued. Regardless of

The only known image of Calogero (Charlie) Carlino, Pete's younger brother. *Courtesy of Karen Filosa.*

how it started, Charlie Carlino and his hired bodyguard, Dominic Ingo, were dead, shot and killed near the banks of the Arkansas River. Dominic Ingo was born on November 25, 1891. He was from Chicago but was born in the same town as Pete Carlino in Lucca Sicula, Sicily.[42] He was married to Jennie Tortorici on September 1, 1917, and the couple had a son named Frank one year later.

Carlo Valenti was traveling with the Dannas and was suspected to have been the bodyguard for the brothers. Charlie Carlino, Dominic Ingo and an unknown accomplice were traveling north from Model, Colorado, when they crossed the bridge. Apparently the cars passed each other and stopped on opposite ends of the bridge. Carlino and Ingo took refuge on the north end of the bridge above the banks of the Arkansas River. This

Baxter Road bridge at the Arkansas River. Charlie Carlino defended the north side of the river as the Danna brothers attacked from the south. *Courtesy of GoogleMaps.*

The Arizona Daily Star

Full Associated Press Report by Leased Wire

VOL. XIV.   NO. 237   TEN PAGES   TUCSON, ARIZONA, TUESDAY MORNING, SEPTEMBER 11, 1923   TEN PAGES   On Trains and at News Stands, 5c a Copy

2 KILLED, MANY WOUNDED IN FIGHT NEAR PUEBLO

Headline of Charlie Carlino's killing. *From the* Arizona Daily Star, *September 11, 1923.*

river is a major tributary to the Mississippi River and actually flows to the state of Arkansas.

Carlino and Ingo defended their stronghold on the north side of the river, and a firefight ensued.[43] They riddled the Danna vehicle with dozens of bullets. Pete Danna was able to rush home in the car to his nearby farm in Vineland to collect more guns and ammunition. While at home, Pete Danna called his *compare* Frank Bacino and had him bring reinforcements and deliver more guns and ammo. Pete Danna, Frank Bacino and their crew returned to the bridge. His brother John and Carlo Valenti stationed themselves on the southern bank of the river and maintained their position. When reinforcements arrived, it was too much for Carlino and Ingo. Outnumbered and outgunned, Charlie Carlino found a fordable section of the river to retreat as he was shot in the back multiple times. Carlino fell face first into the Arkansas River, and his lifeless body floated just downstream and lodged onto a sandbar that had been formed in the center of the river. Dominic Ingo took cover behind a large stump and was shot several times as he rose to fire at the Dannas.

Ingo bled out behind the stump, and the two Danna vehicles fled the scene and returned to their Vineland ranch. After the battle, it was reported that hundreds of bullets had been spent and that the firefight lasted more than two hours. Newspaper reports named Charlie Carlino as one of the deceased, and investigators had found the hat of Dominic Ingo and determined that he purchased it in Chicago. Ingo was not identified until days later. Pueblo County sheriff Sam Thomas responded to several witness accounts alleging that the Dannas were involved in the shootout. Sheriff Thomas arrived at the Danna farm to find John Danna's Ford riddled with thirty-seven bullet holes. John and Pete Danna and Carlo Valenti were arrested and charged with murder.

In December 1923, the Danna brothers and Valenti would stand trial for the murder of Charlie Carlino and Dominic Ingo. The Dannas pleaded not guilty and stated that it was self-defense. The Dannas claimed that Charlie was waiting in ambush for them as they crossed the bridge and that they had sought reinforcements only as a defense measure. Pete Danna stated that Charlie Carlino had visited their farm several times and was trying to persuade them to send Black Hand extortion letters for money to the Dannas' neighbors. Pete Danna stated that he "would rather beg than do that." The true reason for Charlie Carlino's visits to the Danna farm will never be clear. Danna attorney Thomas R. Hoffmire attempted to sway the jury with testimony from four nativist Coloradans who were character witnesses for the Dannas and could testify "to the general reputation of the Danno [*sic*] brothers as peaceful and law abiding citizens."[44] Hoffmire pulled on the heartstrings of the jury and pleaded during closing statements:

> *I ask you gentlemen of the jury, in plain words, are the children of these good Vineland farmers to be nailed to the black hand cross of murder and brigandage? Is it to be broadcasted this evening to the black hand headquarters in Chicago, Buffalo, Cleveland and other places that these good American farmers residing in the breadbasket region of Pueblo County are to be punished for slaying the blackhanders who attacked them?*

In Colorado, the public sentiment against Italians was at its zenith. Hoffmire attempted to sway the Anglo-American jury that the Dannas were different from other immigrant farmers and were "American farmers," while the Carlinos were Black Handers. D.A. Hughes was the prosecuting attorney for the State of Colorado. During his closing statements, Hughes issued a different stance from that given by Hoffmire:

> *Shed no tears for the families of the dead and the families of the living, but shed tears for your own children who are living under a government which is being ignored and overridden by merciless assassins who know no government but that invisible secret government of their own, controlled by hate, malice, and revenge.*

The jury deliberated for nearly thirty hours and split evenly down the middle. The Carlino-Danna case ended in a hung jury.[45] Since it was mid-December, a new trial date needed to be set, but because this trial was the last one of the docket for 1923, the judge dismissed the jury and ordered the Dannas back to jail until a new trial could be scheduled. The Dannas were released on bond and went home awaiting the new trial. The new term was scheduled to begin in late January, but the case was never reopened. The Dannas were free.

The Dannas were free from the U.S. legal system, but there would be a sentencing from another authority that the Sicilian brothers must have known was imminent. Pete and Sam Carlino had lost their little brother, and the Dannas were to blame. Both families were playing a volatile game, with grave consequences hanging in the balance. Wives and children were the collateral damage as stubborn, prideful men staked their claim in this battleground of bootleg territory.

AUTHOR'S PERSPECTIVE

The Baxter Bridge Shootout is such an infamous event that it is still recognized more than ninety years after it occurred. Pete Danna's testimony that Charlie was at their ranch persuading them to send Black Hand letters does not make sense. Black Hand letters were rarely sent after Prohibition began. There was too much money to be made in selling bootleg whiskey compared to extorting local Sicilians. I believe the witness testimony given at the trial was accurate, when it was stated that the two cars passed each other across the bridge and stopped and then the firefight ensued.

Charlie's wife, Calogera (Carrie), and daughter, Charlotte (also called Carrie), moved to New York after he was killed. His daughter lived there for the remainder of her life. I reached out to Charlie's granddaughter Karen Filosa, and she was kind enough to share the only known photo of Charlie Carlino, included in this book. It was a studio photo that had been touched up with watercolors. It was so great to connect with her and talk about our grandfather's past.

Chapter 7

"Vendetta"

Revenge

I n 1924, Pete Carlino moved to Trinidad, Colorado. The family lived at 115 West Fourth Street. They resided in an Anglo-American neighborhood, appearing as a successful, assimilated immigrant family.[46] Pete and Jennie added another son to their family with the birth of Salvatore (Sammy). With five sons and a daughter, Pete Carlino was growing his family while establishing himself in the Trinidad liquor market. He often traveled back east to make alliances in St. Louis, Missouri; Omaha, Nebraska; Milwaukee, Wisconsin; and Chicago. In Chicago, Pete would purchase top-shelf liquor from Al Capone's organization that was smuggled from Canada for his more discerning clientele back home.

Pete's brother-in-law, Carl Mulay, settled in Trinidad with his family to escape the contentious surroundings of Pueblo. Pete Carlino's cousin Frank Parlapiano stayed in Pueblo and distributed Carlino booze from his Pueblo pool hall.

Pete and Sam's associate John Cha (pronounced "kaw") was the new distributor of Carlino booze in Trinidad. Twenty-six-year-old Cha owned a soft drink parlor in downtown that fronted for the distribution of the Carlino product. Cha was born in Colorado shortly after his parents arrived from Italy.

If one were keeping score on the feud between the Dannas and the Carlinos, it would be one-sided. Six Carlino (family or friends) members had been killed compared to zero Dannas. The killing of Pete and Sam Carlino's little brother, Charlie, escalated the vendetta to epic proportions.

Above: Early Trinidad. *Courtesy of the Trinidad Carnegie Library.*

Right: Sammy Carlino, the author's father, 1924. *Courtesy of the Carlino family collection.*

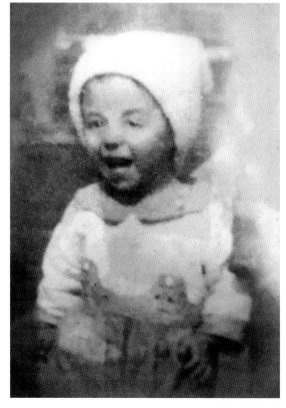

The animosity between families was palpable, and the scores were about to be evened.

On the morning of June 21, 1924, Danna associate Joe Spinuzzi was gunned down at the Pizzutti Roadhouse on the Old Santa Fe Trail. Spinuzzi was a native Coloradan and served during World War I in France. He was also a henchman and bodyguard for the Dannas and helped distribute liquor as well. He was in a card game at Pizzutti's when he was called away from the table to speak to a man outside. Several gunshots were heard, and he was found with five bullet wounds in his abdomen.

Spinuzzi was rushed to the hospital and revealed to his brother Sam that he was called outside by Don Liddo (alias Carl Campinos). Once outside, Liddo jumped aside as Joe Martinelli, Francesco (Frank) Lucia and Vincenzo Colletti appeared around the corner and started shooting at him. He said he fell to the ground when a shot struck below his knee.[47] The three men ran to an awaiting big red car, while Campinos halted for a moment to fire four or five more shots at him. He also stated that Jack DiGrado was driving the car. Jack DiGrado was brother to Ursula DiGrado, who married Vincenzo "Charlie" Guardamondo. The Guardamondos were cousins to Pete Carlino. The Vincenzo Colletti whom Spinuzzi was referring to was Carlino cousin Vincenzo "Charlie" Colletti. (He is not to be confused with Vincenzo "Black Jim" Colletti. Although they are both Pete's cousins with the same name, "Black Jim" Colletti lived in New York at the time and was in Sicily during the time of the murder. He was visiting his mother in Lucca Sicula.)

The police tracked Frank Lucia down and presented him at Spinuzzi's bedside at St. Mary's Hospital for identification. Joe Spinuzzi was too weak to respond. Joe's brother Sam lifted his head to look at Lucia as his face contorted with intense anger, but no words came out. He wanted to talk, but he was too weak to speak. Spinuzzi died shortly thereafter.

Frank Lucia was indicted for the murder of Joe Spinuzzi. During the trial, defense attorney Burris cross-examined Sam Spinuzzi and grilled him for inconsistent testimony. He stated that Sam's testimony at the coroner's inquest differed from that at the trial. Spinuzzi claimed that his statements were different due to fear of retaliation against his mother, sister and himself. Defense attorney John A. Martin objected to Spinuzzi claiming that the four men jumped into a big red car. Until four days before, they had never heard of that testimony. On March 5, 1925, one juror was excused because of a stomach ulcer, and both the prosecution and defense agreed to continue with the trial with only eleven jurors.[48] After careful deliberation, the jury acquitted Frank Lucia for the murder of Joe Spinuzzi.

Frank Lucia had been living in a room rented by a man named Joe Marion.[49] After investigation into the renter's background, the police determined that Joe Marion was actually Frank Parlapiano. Parlapiano was Pete Carlino's cousin on his mother's side. Parlapiano's father, Calogero, and Pete's father, Vito, traveled to America together in 1888. Lucia had been hired to exterminate the Danna brothers' bodyguard and henchman Joe Spinuzzi. The Carlinos were about to systematically remove the Danna lieutenants and bodyguards in the hope of exposing their real target.

Joe Piscopo and his brother-in-law, Jim Giarratano, were at Piscopo's home on July 3, 1924, when a car stopped in front of his house and began firing. Piscopo was on his porch with a friend when the shooting began. According to his daughter, Bonnie, a car slowed to a stop and men began firing at her father.[50] She stated that she saw him jump from the porch and return three shots before collapsing on the lawn. Giarratano was able to grab a shotgun and returned fire through the window, later claiming that he had winged one of the assailants. Piscopo lay dead on his lawn while his wife, Rose, and daughter, Bonnie, stood over him. It was suspected that the Carlinos had hired out-of-town gunmen to exterminate Piscopo. Andrea Lomeli from New York City was admitted to the hospital that evening with gunshot wounds and died on July 4. It was believed that Lomeli had been staying at the same rented house as Frank Lucia.

The Carlino vendettas were enacted, and since Giarratano and Piscopo were accused (but released) of the attempted murder of Carl Mulay and the killing of Vincenzo Urso, they realized that they were both targets.

The Danna farm in Vineland was raided by federal officers and deputies from the Sheriff's Office on April 30, 1925. They were tipped off by an anonymous caller regarding where to find the stills. The Dannas had a manufacturing facility in place that yielded hundreds of gallons of moonshine. Officials seized two thousand gallons of mash and broke up two whiskey stills at their ranch. Sam Danna held off federal officers with a sawed-off shotgun until he could be disarmed. Sam and Tony Danna were both arrested.[51] The discovery and destruction of the Danna stills were a crushing blow to the family's livelihood. James Giarratano was believed to have made the call. He worked closely with Joe Piscopo and the Dannas and knew the location of all of their facilities. It appeared that the Carlinos had pressured Giarratano to switch alliances. Fear for his life as well as his sister Rosa's most likely precipitated this reversal.

On July 16, 1925, Danna family patriarch Giovanni (John) Danna was murdered while working on his crops at their Vineland ranch. Theories abound why he was murdered and who murdered him.[52] Some believe that he was shot by someone hiding in a ditch and the perpetrator was never found, while others believe that the Carlino family had hired a gunman to take out the Danna leader. According to Pete Carlino's son Sam (1924–2002), the Danna incident was precipitated by a disagreement between John Danna and Carlo Marino Sr. over the shared usage of the Bessemer water ditch. (Sam Carlino's explanation has been backed up with articles from the day describing the events.)

Carlo Marino Sr. owned the adjacent property next to the Danna farm and lived there with his son Carlo Jr. and his grandson. The Marinos and Dannas shared the usage of water. Apparently, Marino diverted the water before a specified time, and John Danna angrily approached the elderly man and shoved him to the ground. He warned Marino never to utilize the water before their agreed time or the punishment would be death. Carlo Marino Sr. returned to his house and informed his thirty-three-year-old son Carlo Marino Jr. of the altercation. Marino Jr., avenging his father's honor, approached John Danna from behind and used Danna's own shotgun to kill him. John Danna was shot in the chest at point-blank range. Marino Jr. scurried into the brush to avoid detection from Sam and Pete Danna.[53] The brothers fired several shots into the bushes in hopes of hitting the assailant who had murdered their brother, but they had missed their mark.

The following day, the Dannas exacted their revenge. Carlo Marino Jr.'s cousin Jack Spoone was sitting on the porch of the Marino house when a shot fired from afar struck the seventeen-year-old through the collarbone. Spoone was at the Marino home to do chores when he was shot. The boy had not been involved in the killing of John Danna but was an innocent victim of the vendetta. The wounded Spoone leaped into his automobile and drove three miles to a pool hall in Blende.[54] From there, a doctor and ambulance was sent for and his wounds treated. Jack Spoone died many years later in Pueblo in 1976.

After avenging the insult to his father, Carlo Marino Jr. fled Colorado and hid in the Italian quarter of New Orleans for nearly two years. Carlo Marino Jr. returned to Pueblo on April 19, 1927, and surrendered to the police for the murder of John Danna in 1925. He claimed that "fear of vengeance" kept him from turning himself in sooner.[55] A coroner's jury had found him to be responsible for Danna's death and an arraignment scheduled, but a trial was never set. Marino would never stand trial for John Danna's murder.

Frank Bacino had been shot on two separate occasions and survived both shootings, but he would not survive a third. On April 13, 1926, Frank Bacino was shot in the back while he sat in a chair at his niece Rose Piscopo's Denver property. Bacino was an ally of the Danna brothers, a main distributor of their liquor and a comrade in arms when he resupplied Pete Danna and his brother with guns and ammo during the Baxter Bridge Shootout, which claimed the life of Charlie Carlino. The Carlinos were well aware of the Danna allies, and the death of Pete and Sam's little brother, Charlie, escalated the vendetta.

Frank Bacino was in Denver on April 13, 1926, and was invited to his niece's business for an evening meal.[56] Rose Piscopo, Joe's widow, and her brother Jim Giarratano were hosting Frank Bacino when he was shot. While sitting in a rocking chair with his back to the window, six shots rang out and five hit their target. A .32-caliber revolver was found just outside the window. Police initially believed that it was a Black Hand shooting, but after further investigation, they arrested Rose Piscopo and Jim Giarratano for the murder. Police found .32-caliber shells that could fit the revolver in Jim Giarratano's car. Rose was taken to the office of Assistant Chief of Detectives William Armstrong, where she was confronted by Frank Bacino's brother Charles.[57] Charles intimidated her enough to confess to the killing. She said she planted a sawed-off shotgun in a suitcase about a block away in hopes of diverting suspicion.[58]

Rose Piscopo stated that she had killed Bacino, called her brother Jim into the house to show him the body and begged him to remain silent while being questioned by the police. Piscopo told the police that she was ridding herself of Bacino's unwanted attentions. She declared that Bacino had hounded her with sexual advances for more than fifteen years, and when she told him she was moving to New York, he said he was going to follow her there.

A coroner's jury rejected Rose Piscopo's admission of guilt for the murder of Frank Bacino on April 18, 1926.[59] To add to the peculiar situation, Assistant Chief Armstrong requested to the chief of police that he be removed from the case and reassigned to street duty as a sergeant. It was stated at police headquarters that Armstrong wanted no further connection with the case and that Piscopo's confession was made to shield the real slayer. Rose Piscopo's brother Jim Giarratano was soon the primary suspect and would stand trial for the first-degree murder of Frank Bacino.

On October 1, 1926, James Giarratano was found guilty of the murder of Frank Bacino, and his sister Rose was ruled not guilty. District Attorney Earl Wettengel had been able to prove that Giarratano was the murderer and that Rose was trying to take the blame and gain sympathy from the jury.

Sentencing was scheduled for November, and Judge Henry Bray handed down a life sentence for Giarratano at the state penitentiary in Canon City, Colorado, for the murder of Bacino.[60] Judge Bray overruled a motion for a new trial.[61] Later that evening, District Attorney Earl Wettengel was at home in bed when he heard strange noises outside his bedroom window. He approached the window when a shot rang out, nearly hitting him. He hid behind a dresser and escaped a second shot. Wettengel grabbed his revolver and returned fire. He unleashed two shots at a man fleeing in the darkness but missed his target. Immediately after the incident, he moved his family to spend the night in a hotel in the downtown area.[62] Police investigated whether the attempt on his life was connected to the life sentence handed down to Jim Giarratano earlier that day. Some speculated that Jim Giarratano and Rose Piscopo were blackmailed or bribed to kill Bacino on behalf of the Carlinos. Expecting that Rose's guilty admission and testimony would work toward a lighter sentence, the plan the two had concocted backfired.

John Danna was dead, Frank Bacino was dead, Joe Spinuzzi was dead, Giarratano was serving a life sentence and the Danna brothers had lost their most valuable associate and distributor of their moonshine. The bulk of the Danna empire was about to come crumbling down in the months following Bacino's death.

AUTHOR'S PERSPECTIVE

The year 1924 was a busy one for the Carlinos. My father, Sammy, was born, and quite a few casualties occurred. The killing of John Danna was a pivotal event in the Carlino/Danna struggle. Ironically, the Carlinos were not involved in his killing. Rose Piscopo and James Giarratano killing Bacino at the behest of the Carlinos is certainly a possibility. Threats and pressure can often make a person feel obligated to the task at hand when self-preservation is at stake. I always wondered who fired shots at Earl Wettengel the evening of the sentencing of Giarratano.

Chapter 8

"*Proporzionato Punto*"

SCORE EVEN

Sam Inglese (English) operated saloons, pool halls and speakeasies throughout his life in Colorado. Naturalized in 1904, he had assimilated into the fabric of Pueblo while still keeping his Italian roots. He had several run-ins with the Pueblo police and was once fined $300 for allowing gambling at his First Street saloon in 1910.[63] One day later, he was charged by the Pueblo police for conducting an illegal wine room. In 1921, Sam English and his brother Ben were accused of stealing thirty cases of empty bottles from the New Beer Manufacturing Company (a non-alcoholic brew producer). These bottles were most likely destined to house the homemade whiskey that the Carlino and Danna families were producing at the time. Sam English and Ben were found not guilty, and Sam immediately filed a civil suit for $35,500 in damages to the three corporate officers of the company that had pressed charges against him and his brother. He claimed he had been maliciously prosecuted and that mental anguish, loss of credit and loss of time were worth $35,500 to him. He also asked for a tort judgment, carrying with it a prison sentence in case damages and costs were not paid should he win the suit.[64] This was a bold and audacious lawsuit before the era of frivolous litigation. It was considered, but the suit held no water and was dismissed.

Sam English should have noticed that something was amiss on the afternoon of May 14, 1926. His Monte Carlo Pool Hall was usually bustling with local Italians playing billiards, speaking in their native tongue, debating politics and partaking in the occasional illegal refreshment. That

Friday, the pool hall was unusually quiet. Located on First Street between Main and Santa Fe, the Monte Carlo was a virtual ghost town at 1:30 p.m.

The three remaining Danna brothers traveled together whenever possible. There was a sense of security when the three were united. They drove into town from their ranch so Tony could get a haircut, but there was too long of a wait. The brothers then stopped by Benfatti's pool hall briefly and then drove a few blocks to Sam English's establishment. Pete, Tony and Sam Danna parked their sedan on First Street in front of the Monte Carlo. Sam Danna crawled into the back seat and took the opportunity to catch a nap while his two older brothers conducted business. Pete and Tony Danna stood on the sidewalk and motioned for Sam English to join them.

The three were having a discussion when, without notice, a Hudson Coach materialized from Main Avenue. The tires' squealing woke Sam Danna from the back seat, and he peered into the rear-view mirror of the car. Gunmen brandishing short-barreled shotguns unleashed a fusillade of lead into the unsuspecting trio. Pete and Tony Danna sustained mortal injuries as the shotgun blast tore through their flesh. Sam English dove for cover back into his pool hall as hot buckshot perforated his leg. In haste, Sam Danna hurtled out the door of their sedan and took aim with his revolver at the fleeing Hudson Coach. Just before he could squeeze off a round, he was tackled by a bystander. In an instant, retribution had been served to the Dannas, as Pete and Tony lay dying on First Street in the heart of the bustling business district of Pueblo. It was a bold plan to strike in broad daylight with the potential of dozens of witnesses.

Sam Danna crouched beside his wounded and fading brothers and quietly agonized over their demise. He realized that he had escaped the vengeance that was also meant for him. He also understood that he was the last remaining Danna brother in his family and that each of his siblings had numerous children that no longer had a father. Both brothers were rushed to the hospital immediately after the shooting. Sam Danna accompanied Pete and Tony in the patrol wagon, discussing with them what had just happened. Deathbed testimonies were given to the police before the brothers met their fates. Sam English was admitted to the hospital for his leg wounds and survived.

Immediately following the ambush, the Pueblo police set up roadblocks and formed posses to apprehend the culprits.[65] Reports stated that the suspects were headed toward Walsenburg and had possibly split up. The Hudson car was followed by a second car, a Willys Knight, which was located. Reports indicated that the assassins abandoned their vehicles and resumed their flight in unknown autos. Meanwhile, police departments in Pueblo, Trinidad and Aguilar joined in the net that had been cast for the killers. Roadblocks and spotters had been set up and were equipped with radios to expedite the hunt.

Tony Danna died at 5:40 p.m., with Pete following later that evening. Before they passed, they stated to the police that five men were responsible for the shooting. They said Pete Carlino, Sam Carlino, Carl Mulay, John Mulay Jr. and Pete LaRocca were the malefactors. The Dannas informing the police of the slayers was unimaginable according to the Sicilian code of silence. The brothers had violated one of the most sacred oaths of the Old World. The Dannas must have agreed to name their killers as a last-ditch effort to seek justice through the legal system, knowing that only Sam remained to avenge their deaths.

The police hunt continued throughout the night. Reliable reports tipped the police that Pete LaRocca was hiding in the home of Vic LaRocca at 502 East Evans Avenue. Police surrounded the house and searched it at gunpoint but found nothing.[66] The five suspects were indicted for the murder of Pete and Tony Danna.

Newspapers were reporting numerous tips on the whereabouts of the fugitives. Reports indicated that they were hiding in mine shafts near Walsenburg and that the police were minutes behind them, but they were never located. On May 17, the district attorney, sheriff and police chief threatened censorship of all the official news released because of inaccurate stories concerning the pursuit of the Danna killers. The three entities were trying to curb the false and unreliable reporting of stories (especially from out-of-town newspapers). The authorities feared that a lynching would take place if the accused were caught, and such sensational reports could promote such an occurrence.[67]

Sheriff John J. Marty of Trinidad was investigating an intercepted phone call and traced it to the home of Paul Danna (cousin of the Danna brothers). The call indicated that Pete Carlino and John Mulay Jr. were playing poker at Paul Danna's residence in Aguilar between 12:30 p.m. and 12:45 p.m. Paul Danna was arrested and his residence searched, but nothing was found. Paul Danna told the police that he had been playing cards with Pete Carlino and Mulay at the given time.[68] It was also reported that the duo had motored from Aguilar to Walsenburg with friend Sam Amormino. Aguilar police chief Capirelli learned of the trip from Amormino when he returned home around 3:30 p.m. Two alibis supported Pete's whereabouts. All five suspects had disappeared, and on May 18, the dragnet that had been cast for the group was recalled after all possible clues had been exhausted.

The Danna brothers' funeral was held on May 17, 1926. Hundreds of mourners gathered to pay respects to the brothers who were gunned down just three days prior. A long procession of cars with dozens of flower arrangements adorned their sendoff. At Roselawn Cemetery, Sam stood as the last surviving Danna brother as he watched his siblings lowered into the earth.[69]

About three weeks after Sam Danna buried his brothers, he heard his shepherd dog howling mournfully in the night. Sam's wife and five children were at home when he stepped outside onto his porch to investigate. He ventured further into the darkness, and suddenly the dirt in front of him kicked up a cloud of dust as a bullet narrowly missed him, falling short. He immediately returned fire in the direction of the blast and instantly heard another shot from the opposite direction. Sam claimed that he fired nine shots at the fleeing men as he saw five men return to a car with an awaiting driver.[70] Sam Danna realized that the vendetta on his family was unfulfilled as long as he was alive—he was merely a target from this point on.

AUTHOR'S PERSPECTIVE

The bold murders of Pete and Tony Danna in broad daylight sent a chilling message to any possible rival that Pete and Sam Carlino were ruthless gangsters. The cowardly act of a drive-by shooting was their best chance at taking out all the Danna brothers at once. The alibi set up between Pete Carlino, Paul Danna and Sam Amormino illustrated the planning involved, not only providing two solid alibis immediately following the killings but also an escape plan that allowed five killers to evade a county-wide dragnet.

I learned by speaking with Sam Danna's grandson that many of the Danna children were separated after the murders and sent to orphanages. The families were truly collateral damage in this bootleg war.

Chapter 9

"Giustizia"

JUSTICE

Seventy-five days had passed since the five accused slayers of the Danna brothers disappeared. Colorado governor Clarence Morley announced a $500 reward for the capture of each suspect, with the reward totaling $2,500 for all, augmenting the $1,000 reward offered by the County of Pueblo.[71] Pete and Sam Carlino, Carl Mulay, John Mulay Jr. and Pete LaRocca were believed to have been hiding in Los Angeles. On August 22, Sheriff Sam Thomas of Pueblo never imagined that his quiet Sunday morning would be disrupted with the likes of Pete Carlino strolling through his door. Attorneys ushered Pete LaRocca, Carl Mulay and Pete Carlino into the Sheriff's Office to surrender for the Danna murders. They claimed that they had heard they were charged for a crime and wanted to turn themselves in. Sam Carlino and John Mulay Jr. were still at large.[72] In the late summer, the three were trying to negotiate a bond if they turned themselves in, but the judge would not grant it.[73] The advent of the $3,500 reward most likely precipitated the move to surrender, fearing that a disloyal associate might take advantage of the bounty offered by the county and governor.

On September 3, 1926, just two weeks after Pete Carlino's arrest, the *Pueblo Chieftain* ran a front-page story indicating that imported mafia gunmen had been sent to Pueblo. The article claimed that sixteen gunmen had been brought from Chicago, Detroit and Buffalo, New York,[74] possibly with the hope of intimidating witnesses. The *Chieftain* stated that Pueblo held a national voice within mafia-controlled cities and that all sixteen men were registered killers. "Absolute confirmation" came that the information from the *Chieftain*

Pete Carlino's mugshot. *Courtesy of Denver Police Department, Denver Public Library.*

was accurate. The *Chieftain* also boasted that its news force was kept in constant touch with the activities of the killers. It claimed they were living in residential neighborhoods on the north and south sides of town. The *Pueblo Chieftain* prided itself on publishing sensational stories that the public craved. If the reporting of sixteen hired killers jumping off a train together and running to the aid of Pete Carlino would help its circulation, it would print it. In essence, the name "Carlino" sold newspapers.

The *Chieftain* also pointed out in its September 4 article that imported gunmen in Pueblo hadn't had much success in the past. Dominic Ingo and Vincenzo Urso were cited as the failed hitmen hired to protect Carlo Carlino and Carl Mulay. Ingo was killed protecting Charlie Carlino at the Baxter Bridge Shootout, and Carl Mulay narrowly escaped death when Vincenzo Urso intercepted the lead intended for him. The article had a taunting tone to it, stating that the "imported gunmen's training in Chicago, Detroit, and Buffalo usually aided them little when they faced the mettle of the Pueblo gunmen. And it is rumored that a few of the sixteen newcomers may find the city's climate a warm one."

September 15 was the scheduled arraignment of Carlino, Mulay and LaRocca. Jury selection was slated for November 9, 1926. On the first day of jury selection, Sam Danna tried to enter the courtroom concealing two Colt .45s in his pockets. Before the defendants were brought into the courtroom, the guns were discovered. Did Sam Danna have aspirations of exacting his own form of Sicilian justice in an American courthouse? Or were the two military-issued .45s for his own protection? Captain Aubrey Kelf, commanding officer of Battery C of the Colorado National Guard, stated that one of Sam Danna's .45s had recently been stolen from the armory according to the serial numbers. Judge James A. Parks ruled that all spectators entering the courthouse must surrender all firearms beforehand.[75] Bailiffs frisked all spectators to ensure that there were no guns in the courtroom during the trial.

Judge Parks announced that thirteen jurors would be assigned to the trial. In an unprecedented move, he employed a law passed in 1921 allowing a thirteenth juror to be empaneled to hear all of the evidence so that in case of death, sickness, accident or absence of one juror the case might not result in a mistrial.[76] The thirteenth man was not to have any part in deliberation unless another juror was incapacitated. Because of the high-profile defendants and the threat of jury tampering, Judge Parks was the first to employ this rule allowing a thirteenth juror.

Pete Carlino had lined up a dream team of defense lawyers from that era. Defense attorneys John Barbick, Thomas R. Hoffmire and John A. Martin had their work cut out for them. Carlino, Mulay and LaRocca faced the hangman's noose if convicted. Ironically, it was Thomas R. Hoffmire who had defended John and Pete Danna for the murder of Charlie Carlino and was now representing Pete Carlino this time around. Apparently, Pete was impressed with his tactics and not worried about a conflict of interest.

On the first day of jury selection, not one of the fifteen men examined expressed a conscientious objection to the death penalty.[77] The trial was scheduled to last a period of two weeks. Sam Danna sat at the inside of the rail near the attorneys' tables during jury selection. The defendants' backs turned to him, only a few feet away, must have driven Sam mad. The second day ushered in more prospective jurors as they inched toward their mark of the seventy-one who were summoned. A protest from some of the jurors was directed to the judge about the meals that were being served to the men at lunch.[78] One juror stated, "The meat being served wasn't fit for human consumption and that the jurors were being treated like prisoners." By November 9, there were already eleven jurors picked, and they were expected to be finished selecting by the next day.

Prosecutor Vasco G. Seavey and the Carlino defense team had picked their jury. The *Pueblo Chieftain* touted the trial as "one of the local court sensations of the year." The Pueblo courthouse was filled to capacity, and a buzz of electricity flowed through the crowd. The Carlino-Danna case was exhilarating to the Pueblo locals, and the ones who were not lucky enough to get a seat in the courtroom lived vicariously through the titillating reports the *Pueblo Chieftain* turned out every day.

Thomas R. Hoffmire, Pueblo defense attorney. *Courtesy of Wikimedia Commons.*

Throughout the trial, Pete Carlino, Carl Mulay and Pete LaRocca sat stoned-face and listened to monotonous testimony to the events that led up to the Danna brothers' slaying. It was not until Sam Danna was scheduled to take the stand that the three defendants sat up to take notice. The mere fact that Sam Danna was going through with testifying against his countrymen was unheard of in their culture. Not only had Sam Danna identified his brothers' slayers to the police, but he was also about to swear on a Bible in a courtroom that the Carlino gang was liable.

Pete Carlino and his crew must have felt uneasy with the foreboding possibility of being hanged, as well as the likelihood of his brother Sam and John Mulay Jr. being captured and convicted as well. When Sam Danna took the stand, the three defendants glanced at one another and exchanged smiles. Was this done to rattle the witness? Or was it because they knew that Sam Danna had violated the most sacred of oaths of the *Onorata Società*? Regardless, Sam Danna had just signed his predestined order of death, *farlo fuori* ("kill him").

Unlike most Sicilians of this era who were sworn to an oath of amnesia, Sam Danna took the stand and began giving his versions of the events on May 14, 1926. He must have thought it was his only opportunity to at least balance the scorecard and possibly put his family's nemeses away for good. In Sam's mind, having Pete Carlino and his gang convicted and hanged would allow him to return to his family. But on the other hand, what if he were freed? With more than twenty nieces and nephews, as well as his own children to look after, Sam would have to make his farm provide for twenty-five people. Sam Danna spoke little English and required a translator to testify for the trial.

It was November 20, and ironically, the Danna-Carlino trial was occurring at the same time James Giarratano was being sentenced to life in prison up in Denver for the murder of Danna associate Frank Bacino.[79] Giarratano's motion for a new trial was overruled by Judge Bray. For most of the jurors in Pueblo, spending a Saturday night deliberating a case was not their idea of a night on the town. The jury would deliberate more than sixteen hours and vote a total of seven times before they reached a verdict. On Sunday afternoon at 2:00 p.m., the courtroom was filled to capacity to hear the verdict. The families of all three men on trial were present in the courtroom. Sam Danna and his family were at home awaiting word. Once the verdict was handed to the judge from the jury, a pin drop could have been heard. Judge Parks handed the decision to Clerk Nichols, who delivered the verdict in a stentorian voice: "Not guilty!" The Pueblo jury agreed that Pete Carlino, Carl Mulay and Pete LaRocca were not guilty of killing the Danna brothers.

The courtroom erupted in cheers as the three defendants hugged and kissed one another typical of elated Sicilians. Handshakes and pats on the back subsided once Judge Parks called order to the courtroom. The trial was over, but the jury was about to have its say in what transpired the last ten days.

After giving the verdict, the foreman of the jury presented to the court a statement that has never been equaled in Pueblo judiciary history, saying to court officials that the members of the jury resented the alibi statement and the defense and based their verdict solely on the lack of evidence to convict:

> *We, the jury, in the case wherein Pete Carlino, Carlo Mulay, and Pete LaRocca were charged with the murder of Pete and Tony Danna, in which we have just returned a verdict of not guilty, resent as a reflection on the intelligence of the court and jury the introduction of a mass of what we consider perjured testimony in support of a false alibi. We wish to further state that in considering the case no attention was paid by us whatsoever to the alibi and our verdict was reached solely on what we considered insufficient evidence on the part of the state to prove to us beyond a reasonable doubt the presence of the defendants in the car from which the shots were fired.*
>
> *Signed S.A. Walker "Foreman"*

In essence, the jury disregarded the defense's alibi testimony, suspecting that the witnesses had given false testimony. The acquittal decision was based solely on a lack of evidence from the prosecution. Ironically, the jury had been given instructions that the alibis *were* a legitimate defense.[80] The prosecution did not have any other evidence besides the testimony of the Danna brothers that Carlino and his crew were the culprits.

AUTHOR'S PERSPECTIVE

I always pondered what would have occurred if Sam Danna had been able to use the two .45-caliber pistols he kept hidden in his pockets. I truly believe that they were not merely for self-defense. The security procedures that we have to endure today are quite a bit different than they were ninety-five years ago.

It was interesting to see that this trial had two events that had never happened before. First, a thirteenth juror was assigned to the trial in case of jury tampering, and second, the jury rejected the defense's strategy of relying on alibi testimony. This would not be the last trial where a Carlino will be involved in a "first" that happens during a murder trial.

Chapter 10

"Estremità Sciolte"

LOOSE ENDS

After the Danna trial, the Carlinos' bootlegging business soared and raised the brothers to be crowned the undisputed liquor lords of the southern half of the state. Pete had earned the nickname the "Al Capone of Southern Colorado." In 1926, Pete Carlino was still living at 115 West Fourth Street in Trinidad. Across the Purgatoire River, brother Sam and his family were at 313 Topeka Avenue. The remainder of 1926 and throughout 1927 saw little bloodshed. The Carlino brothers expanded their markets north through Colorado Springs and by 1927 were moving their whiskeys into the Denver marketplace. Pete had purchased a Duesenberg sedan, as well as a racehorse in Chicago. Pete and Sam adorned their wives with diamond jewelry and luxurious fur coats. The Carlino brothers spent money on frivolous material items that would come back to haunt them in the coming years.

Sam Danna still lived on his family's Vineland farm and was struggling to take care of his wife and five children, as well as many of his brothers' children. Some of the Danna children were sent to orphanages. On April 19, 1927, neighbor Carlo (Calogero) Marino Jr. turned himself in to the Pueblo Police Department. He returned to "face the music" in Pueblo for the murder of John Danna in 1925. Marino had hid out in the Italian Quarter of New Orleans until he had gotten word that the Danna brothers had been killed and that Sam Danna was no longer a threat. The threat of a Danna shotgun worried Marino far more than the Colorado judicial system. Although a coroner's jury found enough evidence to arrest Marino, he never stood trial for John Danna's murder.

By 1927, Pete Carlino was making plans to move his family to Denver. Jennie was pregnant with her seventh child. Three-year-old daughter Carrie had died in 1925, and the couple was ready to have another *bambino*. In 1927, Pete moved his family to 3648 Alcott Street in the Potter Highland neighborhood in North Denver. Sam was still in Trinidad but was making plans to move his family to San Bernardino in California. In August 1928, Jennie gave birth to their sixth son. The boy was named Pietro Antonio Jr. (Peter Jr.) On November 17, 1928, Pete and Jennie bought a palatial home at 3357 Federal Boulevard. The title to the house was placed in Jennie's name.

The Carlino brothers had one "loose end" to tie up before their vendetta with the Dannas was complete. On the afternoon of October 10, 1928, Sam Danna was riding his beet puller when a barrage of machine gun fire sprayed his vicinity. A swiftly moving vehicle unleashed a torrent of lead targeting the last surviving Danna brother. A bullet lodged in the chest of Sam as he fell to the ground, and he fruitlessly returned fire at the fleeing vehicle with his .45 automatic pistol. The bullet, just three inches from his heart, was first thought to be a life-threatening wound, but Sam Danna survived the assassination attempt. Five days after Sam was shot, he was provided with armed guards as a security measure.[81] The night before, someone was lurking outside his hospital room using flashlights to peer inside. Hospital officials feared another attempt on his life and provided the extra security. Sam recovered and eventually returned to his ranch, but he never felt safe outside his own home.

Pete Carlino had two cousins joining their crew, Ignazio Vaccaro and Peter Carlino (Paulo Carlino's son). For the sake of clarity, cousin Peter Carlino will be referred to as Rudy Constantino, as cousin Peter would eventually change his name to Rudy in 1930. Rudy's father, Paulo Carlino, and Vito Carlino were brothers. Rudy was first cousins with Pete and Sam. Ignazio Vaccaro arrived from New York after he had married Pietrina Camilleri. Vaccaro and Constantino both had criminal records in their past.[82] Vaccaro was arrested for horse thieving in 1918 along with Rudy's brother Stefano.[83] Rudy Constantino was arrested for safe cracking at the Swift meatpacking company and two post office robberies in 1922.[84] In the Sicilian tradition, Pete surrounded himself with family members he could trust. One of Ignazio Vaccaro's duties was to protect Pete Carlino as his bodyguard.

Pete and Sam Carlino's cousin Rudy Constantino was married to Anna Riggio on January 14, 1929. At the time of their marriage, his birth name

Left: Ignazio Vaccaro and Pietrina (Pat) Vaccaro's wedding photo. *Courtesy of the Carlino family collection.*

Right: Anna Riggio Carlino, Rudy Constantino (Peter Carlino), Sammy Carlino (ring bearer) and Josie Carlino (flower girl). *Courtesy of the Carlino family collection.*

was Pete Carlino. His cousins Pete and Sam's young children would have a role in the wedding party. Pete's young boy, Sammy, would be the ring bearer, and Sam's daughter, Josie, would be the flower girl.

Four months after his marriage to Anna Riggio, Rudy would be on the run, wanted for murder. Allegedly, on April 10, 1929, Rudy and his brother-in-law, Jimmy Riggio, coerced Ralph and Mary Solano into their car; what followed was a bizarre turn of events.[85] Ralph and Mary Solano were each shot three times and left for dead on the side of the roadway. Ralph Solano died from his wounds, but Mary stayed alive long enough to inform the police of their slayers. Police suspected that the killing was a bootleg-related hit. Newspapers referenced a family feud in Pueblo, but not many details were given. Ralph Solano worked as a miner and a baker, and his seventeen-year-old wife, Mary, was the daughter of Carlo (Calogero) Marino Jr., who was suspected of killing John Danna but was never brought to trial. Newspapers and books have incorrectly reported that Mary Solano was the daughter of Frank Bacino.

Rudy Constantino (Peter Carlino), Trinidad, 1921. *Courtesy of the Carlino family collection.*

Mary initially refused to name her assailants, but as she inched closer to death, she decided to break the Sicilian code of silence. According to Mary Solano, Rudy Constantino (Pete Carlino) and his brother-in-law, Jimmy Riggio, offered to take them for a ride in their automobile. The four were traveling on the El Moro highway outside Trinidad.[86] Jimmy Riggio was driving, and after a short time, her husband, Ralph, began to feel uneasy. When the two wanted out of the vehicle, Constantino pulled a gun and shot them each three times. The couple was dumped on the roadside and presumed to be dead. Early the following morning, a passerby named Frank Williams discovered the two bodies along the road about a quarter mile west of El Moro. One headline stated, "Rum Runners Kill Husband and Wife."

Left: Sam Carlino and Rudy Constantino. *Courtesy of the Carlino family collection.*

Right: Jimmy Riggio, Rudy Constantino's brother-in-law. *Courtesy of the Carlino family collection.*

Before Mary Marino married Ralph Solano, she had made the headlines in the Pueblo area when she disappeared on July 9, 1927.[87] She was reported kidnapped and was later found in New Mexico unharmed, living with her abductor. The abduction was not initially reported due to their fear of reprisal from their unknown enemies. It is unclear if the abductor was Ralph Solano or if she had left Colorado on her own accord.

Four days after the deaths of Ralph and Mary Solano, police reported that a coroner's jury found Peter Carlino and Jimmy Riggio responsible for the deaths of the couple.[88] A verdict was reached after five witnesses testified at the coroner's inquest. Peter Carlino disappeared and would change his name to Rudy Constantino. He would return one year later and continue his bootleg activities working for his cousins Pete and Sam Carlino. Jimmy Riggio fled Colorado and was presumed to have relocated in Los Angeles. The motive behind the murder remains a mystery.

It had been two years since Sam Danna was shot while tending his beet puller on his Vineland ranch. Recovered from his near fatal chest wound, Sam was always cautious and wary of his surroundings and the people with whom he associated. On the night of May 6, 1930, Sam

Rudy Constantino and Jimmy Canzoneri. *Courtesy of the Carlino family collection.*

Danna was convinced by an unidentified person to venture away from the security of his ranch and meet with someone in Bessemer Alley in Pueblo. Was the promise of exacting revenge against the Carlinos enough to lure Sam from his home? His trust in this unknown friend proved to be fatal, as three shotgun blasts tore through his back at point-blank range, killing him instantly. Police initially thought he was "taken for a ride" and his body dumped in the alley, but after further investigation, it was determined that he was shot and killed in the spot where he was discovered.[89] A loaded handgun was tucked in his pants, and it was believed he was killed with his own shotgun.

The feud that had begun eight years earlier had come to its conclusion. The Carlinos had lost many battles against the Dannas but eventually won the war. Both families lost friends and relatives, children were orphaned and split up and many were separated among strangers. The Carlino brothers had won their conflict against the Dannas and executed the vendetta, but at what cost?

AUTHOR'S PERSPECTIVE

Rudy Constantino was an interesting figure. He died before I was born, but all of my older cousins recall his gregarious nature and charm. He would visit from Los Angeles, and everyone loved him. Little did they know his sordid past. My older cousins were astounded when I told them why he changed his name.

My dad was a big car buff. He could look at any old car from a distance and correctly call out the make, model and sometimes the year of the vehicle. He told me that Pete had bought a Duesenberg, and I was in disbelief. The cost of a Duesenberg was close to $5,000 in 1927. It was one of the most expensive cars in the world. The house they purchased on Federal Boulevard was nearly the same price. My dad recalled the swing of fortune and failure during his early childhood due to Pete's poor money management.

Chapter 11

"La Convenzione"

THE CONVENTION

By March 1929, Pete and Jennie had settled into their palatial home on Federal Boulevard in North Denver. The upscale neighborhood was quite different from the farm they once tended outside Pueblo. Pete had sold the Duesenberg and bought a more practical 1929 Dodge Senior sedan. The three older sons of Pete and Jennie were dealing with the pressures of moving to a new neighborhood. The boys had to endure sarcastic insults from classmates at school and were ridiculed by their teachers for their father's notoriety. All six boys would eventually learn how to defend themselves, but brothers Joe and Chuck were the toughest, as both would be successful boxers later in their lives.

Pete's eldest son, Victor, was a talented musician who played violin and guitar. Pete bought him a rare Stradivarius copy violin made in Italy in the late 1700s. It was a cherished gift that he would keep his entire lifetime and was eventually passed down to the next generation. Sundays were family days, and often Sam's family would join together at Pete's house for a pasta dinner. Jennie would not use meatballs in her sauce (called gravy), but would instead use chuck roast. According to Jennie it imparted a better flavor to the tomato sauce. Sam's wife, Josephine, preferred meatballs and sausage in her pasta sauce but would use the chuck roast if desired.[90]

Jennie hired fifteen-year-old Mary Cacciatore as a maid to help her with her young boys. Mary's family lived on the same street as the Mauro family in Aguilar, Colorado. Her neighbor, Bruno Mauro, was a sixteen-year-old

Above: Pete and Jennie's six boys—Joe, Sammy, Steve, Pete Jr., Vic and Chuck—at the Federal Boulevard house, Denver, Colorado, 1930. *Courtesy of the Carlino family collection.*

Left: Vic Carlino holding his Stradivarius copy violin, Denver, 1930. *Courtesy of the Carlino family collection.*

driver for the Carlino brothers. Mauro's duties included delivering sugar beets to be distilled into moonshine, tending the whiskey stills and transporting barrels of the finished product to their suppliers.

On March 6, 1929, seventeen-year-old Charles Mauro (Bruno Mauro's brother) was driving a new truck laden with fifty-five kegs of moonshine.[91] The "Sugar Moon" was on its way to Denver when two federal prohibition agents stopped him six miles south of Littleton on the Denver–Colorado Springs road. Sam Carlino and associate Sam Cefalu were following the truck in Sam's car as "backup" in case of a hijacking. Federal agents Martin Brink and Charles Crooks arrested all three men. The new truck carrying the kegs of whiskey was confiscated, as was Sam's car.

Pete Jr., two years old, Denver, 1930. *Courtesy of the Carlino family collection.*

The seizure of the Carlino brothers' truckload of whiskey proved to be the biggest bust in several months. The agents put a dent in the supply chain that was destined for the Denver marketplace. Sam Cefalu and his wife, Ester, had recently been convicted of dry law violations, and he was sentenced to serve nine months and was fined $500. Ester was given four months and a $1,000 fine. Cefalu was appealing his case at the time of his arrest with Sam Carlino and Charles Mauro. The confiscation of their new truck, as well as the barrels of moonshine, was a heavy loss for the Carlino brothers' operation. The cost of being incarcerated and bribes paid to public officials, as well as attorney fees, added to their burden. By the end of 1929, the stock market had crashed, and the Depression had officially begun.

On January 24, 1930, Carlino associates John Cha and Jimmy Canzoneri were ambushed, and Canzoneri was riddled with buckshot and died. Cha was wounded but survived. He lay still on the ground and played dead. Newspapers stated that gang warfare was the motive for the attack. The two were near an abandoned coal camp three miles outside Trinidad, changing a flat tire on their automobile. Several months before the ambush, John Cha's house was bombed in Trinidad, but Cha and his wife, Rosa, were unharmed in the blast.[92]

John Cha, Paul Danna and Jimmy Canzoneri, Colorado, 1929. *Courtesy of Paul D'anna.*

The Department of Justice had agents from its Bureau of Prohibition scouring the countryside sniffing out stills and making arrests. In 1930, the DOJ assigned an aggressive agent to patrol the southern section of the state.

Dale Frances Kearney was born in Minnesota in 1900 and was a decorated World War I veteran. He had the tenacity of a pit bull and had only been with the Bureau of Prohibition for thirteen months. He was responsible for more than twenty arrests in the Walsenburg area. He preferred to work alone and rarely had backup from another officer or agency. In June 1930, he confiscated a huge whiskey still and arrested John Kajfosz for moonshining in Trinidad.[93] Kajfosz was born in 1885 in Poland and was a member of the local Masonic Lodge, as well as the reputed head of the local booze syndicate. He supplied alcohol to a large part of Southern Colorado. Since Kajfosz's arrest, Kearney had noted that he had been trailed constantly.

Dale Kearney, Bureau of Prohibition agent, killed while investigating bootleggers in Trinidad, Colorado, 1930. *Courtesy of the Bureau of Alcohol, Tobacco, Firearms and Explosives.*

Kearney had received threatening letters concerning his investigations. On July 6, 1930, acting on a tip, Dale Kearney drove from Trinidad to Aguilar, where he had car trouble. While in town, he spoke with a stranger in a diner about chasing down some bootleggers. Just after midnight, he was returning to his vehicle when four shotgun blasts tore into his body, killing him instantly. His assailant ambushed him in the dark, hiding behind a wooden fence.[94] He was the first federal agent to be killed in the line of duty in Colorado, and his death spurred an onslaught of enforcement from all federal agencies.

A week after his death, federal officers padlocked alleged bootlegging "joints" and suspected liquor gang hangouts throughout Southern Colorado.[95] A concerted effort was made to find the murderer of Dale Kearney, but no clues were ever discovered. The assassination of Kearney prompted federal authorities to implement a strategy never attempted before in Colorado. The plan was twofold: discover Kearney's assassin and insert an undercover federal agent into an established bootlegging operation to learn the details of how the organization operated. Within weeks, the Department of Justice had picked an agent with an Italian background and nerves of steel. The DOJ would never discover who was responsible for Dale Kearney's death, but its undercover agent would help take down the biggest organized bootlegging operation in Colorado.

Lawrence Baldesareli was supposedly a Chicago gunman, but he was actually a federal agent working for the U.S. Attorney's Office. In

August 1930, Baldesareli worked his way into Colorado's most significant organized crime family. He had been introduced to Pete Carlino by John Cha in Trinidad. Within two months, he had gained the trust of Pete enough for him to be placed as bodyguard for his brother Sam Carlino. In an unprecedented move, Pete allowed an outsider into the inner circle of the Carlino family. Pete was impressed with Baldesareli's abilities with a gun and the intellect that he possessed. The inner secrets of the Carlino operation were now being directly related to the Department of Justice and U.S. Attorney Ralph Carr.

Pete Carlino had moved his business into the Denver territory and was trying to control the Northern Colorado liquor market. He had threatened and intimidated many of the local bootleggers and at times had hijacked their supplies. He had threatened to bomb their moonshine stills if they did not agree to work with him.

Pete wanted to organize an alliance with other bootleggers in the area and put an end to the slashing of liquor prices. Supply was outpacing demand of the product being distilled, and the prices of moonshine were dropping. In 1926, locally distilled moonshine was three dollars per pint; by 1931, the same pint of shine was costing only seven dollars per gallon and one dollar per pint.

Early bootleggers gathering in 1929. John Cha, with his arm around Pete Carlino, and Joe Roma are seen here side by side in the middle row. Paul Danna, wearing a fedora hat, is in the top row next to sidekick Jimmy Canzoneri, also with a hat. *Courtesy of Susan Carlino Evanoff.*

Pete Carlino wanted to organize a meeting to forge a "bootleggers' trust" and fix the price at ten dollars per gallon and two dollars per pint. In addition to the two-dollar price, Pete Carlino wanted twenty-five cents of every gallon sold to go into a defense fund to help any bootleggers caught pay their attorney fees. Pete devised the plan of the Bootleggers Convention and set a meeting for nearly thirty attendees. The La Palamarte Roadhouse at 6601 West Thirty-Eighth Avenue in Wheat Ridge hosted the event on January 24, 1931.

Such gatherings had occurred in the past, but none was as encompassing as the meeting planned for January 24. The afternoon of the assemblage, Police Captain of Detectives Albert T. Clarke received a tip that the Bootleggers Convention would be occurring at the Palamarte later that evening. Undercover agent Lawrence Baldesareli had tipped the police to the meeting in the hopes of breaking up a union of bootleggers that could have formed a trust and organized the whiskey peddlers.

Joe Roma, leader of the North Denver faction of the bootlegging operation, was conspicuously absent, along with his lieutenants, the Smaldone brothers. Roma's past is quite hazy. He claimed that he was born in San Francisco but was believed to have been born in Calabria in the southern section of Italy. Rumors that he was connected to the Calabrian faction of the mafia abound, but there is so little we really know of his past.

The Carlinos had formed an alliance with Roma and the Smaldones. In January 1931, the Carlinos were meeting with Raffaele Smaldone. Members of the Carlino gang were photographed with Raffaele. It was suspicious that Joe Roma and the Smaldone brothers were absent from the biggest gathering of bootleggers in the city's history.

The meeting had only just begun when twenty-three police officers armed with machine guns surrounded all three exits of the building. Twenty-nine bootleggers, including Pete and Sam Carlino, were arrested for vagrancy and held in the Denver jail. The men told the police that they were just gathering for a chicken dinner. Almost every man attending had prior arrests, and some had as many as twenty to their name. The arraignment was set for Monday, February 2, and the trial was set for February 9 in Golden, Colorado. The meeting led to the apprehension of twenty-nine bootleggers, with nine belonging to the Carlino gang.[96] All the men gave Denver addresses, but police suspected that many were from Pueblo and other Southern Colorado cities. Three of the accused decided to give statements to the police. Details of why the meeting was called were

Above: Rudy Constantino, Joe Petralia, a young boy who could be Clarence Smaldone, Sam Carlino, a young boy who could be Ralph Smaldone Jr., Dan Riggio and a man who could be Raffaele Smaldone, Denver, Colorado, January 1931. *Courtesy of the Carlino family collection.*

Left: Sam Carlino, a young boy who could be Ralph Smaldone Jr., Rudy Constantino, Joe Petralia and a man who could be Raffaele Smaldone, Denver, Colorado, January 1931. *Courtesy of the Carlino family collection.*

IN THIS PAPER YOU WILL FIND DAILY THE TELEGRAPHIC SERVICES OF THE ASSOCIATED PRESS, NEW YORK TIMES, CHICAGO TRIBUNE, UNIVERSAL SERVICE, INTERNATIONAL NEWS, CONSOLIDATED PRESS AND UNITED PRESS. NO OTHER NEWSPAPER IN THE WORLD HAS ALL OF THESE SERVICES

POLICE ARMED WITH MACHINE GUNS RAID BOOTLEG CONVENTION AND ARREST 29 MEN

THE DENVER POST

92 PAGES   DENVER, COLO., SUNDAY MORNING, JAN. 25, 1931

DENVER HAS FEWER OUT OF WORK THAN OTHER BIG CITIES

PLOT OF SOUTHERN COLORADO GANG TO INVADE DENVER FOUND

Local Bootleggers Said to Have Sought Truce With Leader of Liquor Ring, Who Threatened Underworld War

relayed to Denver detectives by bootleggers Mike Seganti, H. Hall and Jerry Nevan (Newman).

Captain Clarke made an impassioned statement to the press directed at the gangsters.[97] "Get out and stay out of Denver," he warned. "Denver police are ready for you guntoters. You start anything and police will finish you with machine guns. Denver has existed without gangs. It will exist without gangs in the future. One funny move from any of you and you'll wish you had never heard of Denver."

Pete Carlino was approached by Denver police chief Richard "Diamond Dick" Reed with a deal. Reed bargained with Pete to drop the charges of vagrancy if he would voluntarily leave the state of Colorado. Pete agreed and was released but was given a warning: if he was seen in public again, he would be re-arrested. Just one hour after his release, Pete was waiting in the patrol wagon room of the Denver Police Department, where he was arrested again for vagrancy. Reed was known as being a corrupt police chief, as well as a stooge for Mayor Stapleton.

Following is a summarized and annotated list of the arrested men, attained by the *Denver Post*:

- Pete Carlino (forty-three), 3357 Federal Boulevard, Denver, Salesman, Carlino Faction
- Sam Carlino (thirty-nine), 3485 West Thirty-Third Avenue, Denver, Salesman, Carlino Faction
- Danny Colletti (nineteen), 3338 Tejon Street, Denver, Laborer, Carlino Faction
- Joe Barry (Borello) (thirty-five), 3900 Tejon Street, Denver, Salesman, Carlino Faction

This page, top: Pete Carlino's mugshot. *Courtesy of the Denver Police Department, Denver Public Library.*

This page, bottom: Police chief warns bootleggers as Pete Carlino agrees to leave the state of Colorado if freed. *From the* Denver Post, *Denver Public Library.*

Opposite: Bootleggers Convention headline from *Denver Post*, January 25, 1931.

- Joe Ferraro (thirty-five), Luna Hotel, Denver, Laborer, Carlino Faction
- Sam Cefalu (thirty-three), 4118 Shoshone Street, Denver, Truck Driver, Carlino Faction
- Carl Dotson (thirty-seven), 2320 Glenarm Place, Denver, Carlino Faction
- J.L. Brownie (thirty-one), 1734 Washington Street, Denver, Laborer, Carlino Faction
- Chick Massey, Denver
- Ross Camino (thirty-two), 3910 Jason Street, Denver
- A. Mistretta (forty-five), 45 Edgewater Street, Denver, Salesman
- George Ball (forty), 3355 Shoshone Street, Denver
- Carl Lombardi (thirty-three), 3356 Shoshone Street, Denver, Farmer
- George Freeman (twenty-seven), 4007 Vallejo Street, Denver, Laborer
- James Marino (twenty-four), 3167 Navajo Street, Printer
- Frank Moreno (thirty-two), 1429 Cherokee Street, Clerk
- George Iello (twenty-five), 3916 Tejon Street, Denver, Salesman
- Tony Muro (thirty-six), 2104 West Thirty-Fourth Avenue, Denver, Painter
- Jack Ursetta (thirty-eight), 3614 Navajo Street, Denver, Barber
- L. Miller (thirty-five), 2811 West Fourteenth Avenue, Denver, Plumber
- Fonzie Pitts (twenty-seven), 3638 Tejon Street, Denver
- Ross Benaggio (twenty-seven), 2143 West Twenty-Ninth Avenue, Denver, Mechanic
- Mike Guaraci (twenty-two), 3638 Tejon Street, Denver, Truck Driver
- Charles Lombardo (twenty-two), 2329 West Twenty-Ninth Avenue, Denver, Mechanic
- F. Mina (forty-two), 4086 Shoshone Street, Laborer
- S. Silvestro (thirty-eight), 3311 Tejon Street, Denver, Salesman
- Mike Seganti (twenty-six), 4040 Shoshone Street, Denver, Merchant, Spoke to Police, No Charges
- H. Hall (thirty-three), Dover Hotel, Denver, Mechanic, Spoke to Police, No Charges
- Jerry Nevan (Newman) (twenty-six), 2731 West Twenty-First Street, Denver, Salesman Spoke to Police, No Charges

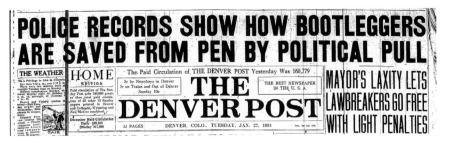

Headline from the *Denver Post* exposing the paid political protection for bootleggers from elected officials. *From the* Denver Post, *January 27, 1931, Denver Public Library.*

On February 4, 1931, Judge Walter E. White released eleven bootleggers, including Pete and Sam Carlino, Joe Ferraro and Dan Colletti, as well as seven others. White stated, "Perhaps their past reputation has not been the best, but nothing definite has been shown against them." Sam was rearrested immediately and charged with carrying a concealed handgun at the time of the Bootleggers Convention.[98]

Denver mayor Benjamin F. Stapleton was singled out in the *Denver Post* as instigating the suspended sentences handed down from Judge White.[99] The *Post* stated that "political pull and graft make most of the bootleggers virtually immune to punishment.…Political pull is the *monkeywrench* that has been slipped into the law enforcement machinery at Denver's city hall to nullify prohibition laws and ordinances.…Records of the men arrested in the Police raid Saturday on the alleged Bootleggers Convention reek with such notations as 'fine suspended,' 'case dismissed' or 'no disposition of case.'" The *Denver Post* was clearly identifying that public officials were entrenched in the web of organized crime and, by their association with them, were facilitating their protection from the laws.

Ike Merritt was the secretary for Mayor Stapleton when Merritt was caught embezzling $26,000 from the mayor's contingent fund.[100] He was convicted on February 19, 1931. From his jail cell, he cut loose with a statement to the press exposing the rottenness and corruption within city hall:[101]

"Since I left my job at the city hall I have seen with my own eyes a payoff man collect money to be turned over to a city official." He also stated, "I know the name and address of a man used by Chief of Police Reed to tap telephone wires, and this has been done a number of times.…If I have to be the goat for other people, and if money actually was misappropriated from the Mayor's contingent fund, I intend to make it my business to see

the real man doesn't escape punishment." Merritt was outspoken in his denunciation of Mayor Stapleton, who, he says "promised to help me out" and then threw all responsibility for the contingent fund upon him. "The Mayor is a damned liar."

Mayor Ben Stapleton was a Democrat and a member of the local Ku Klux Klan in Denver (member no. 1128).[102] The Klan helped establish him as mayor in 1923. He appointed William Candlish as police chief, who was also a member of the KKK. Stapleton lost his bid for another mayoral term in May 1931 but would return to regain his throne in the 1935 election. The Denver International Airport was named after him until its closure in 1995. In 2018, residents who live in the Stapleton neighborhood in Denver were pushing to have the named changed because of his Ku Klux Klan affiliation.

AUTHOR'S PERSPECTIVE

The group photo of Pete Carlino, Joe Roma, Paul Danna, Gaetano Danna, John Cha and others is such a significant piece of history. My cousin Susan was so kind to share the photograph with everyone for the book. It is a one-of-a-kind photo that shows the connection between these characters as early as 1929.

It was not a coincidence that Roma and the Smaldone brothers were absent from the Bootleggers Convention. I believe that once the Baldesareli tip was received at the Denver Police Station, a call was placed to Joe Roma warning him about the impending raid. The political graft is apparent when Judge White released most of the men apprehended at the meeting.

My dad always enjoyed Aunt Josie's spaghetti sauce more than his mother's, he told me. He did not like the taste of the chuck roast that Jennie would put in the sauce. When my dad married my mom, he had Aunt Josie teach her how to make the Sicilian-style gravy he was accustomed to. My mom was from Arkansas and had never made spaghetti sauce before she met my dad. Between Aunt Pat and Aunt Josie teaching her, she caught on quickly and became a very good Italian cook.

Chapter 12

"La Bomba"

The Bomb

On February 15, 1931, Carlino associate Joe Borello (Barry) was shot and wounded in front of his house in Denver.[103] Police questioned him at St. Joseph's Hospital regarding the identity of the two would-be assassins, but Borello gave no information. Three days later, Joe Borello's boss, Pete Carlino, was standing on a corner at Tejon Street in Denver when a car slowed down and fired four shots at him. All four shots missed their mark as Pete scurried to safety. Pete's cousins Joe Ferraro, Dan Colletti and Joe Petralia were picked up by police and questioned after the shooting but released.

Captain Clark stated, "We have information three professional killers were brought here recently to take a hand in the booze war," adding, "We have a hint as to their identity, but have been unable to locate their hideout." Three eastern gunmen who were reported to have been imported to "make away with" (i.e., kill) five bootleggers marked for death were sought by police. Clark added, "Carlino and Barry know who their assailants are, but are remained mum as to the identity of the assailants."

The Carlino gang was under attack from all sides. On February 18, Pete's bodyguard, Ignazio Vaccaro, disappeared on his way to Denver from Trinidad. He received a call from Denver informing him that an assassination attempt on Pete had occurred that day. He was told to return immediately.[104] He was last seen in Pueblo on February 18, 1931. His car was found a few days later on an isolated road twenty-two miles east of Colorado Springs. His handgun was on the seat, and there was no sign of a struggle. Police informants heard that he had been killed, stuffed into a furnace and burned. His wife, Pietrina, was in Denver at the time of his disappearance. Carlino associate John Cha and his wife, Rose, disappeared at the same time Vaccaro was leaving for Denver. They were also on their way to Denver to aid Pete Carlino.

Pete knew that he and his crew were marked men and would have to be cautious if they wanted to survive this latest onslaught of mob violence. For the past two years, the Carlino brothers had endured heavy losses to their bootleg business by law enforcement and rival gangs. The Carlinos lost fifty-five kegs of whiskey in one stop by Prohibition agents and a whiskey still they operated on East Sixteenth Street that was blown up by rival gangsters. Carlino associate Joe Borello's home was raided by the police, and a cache of weapons was seized.

On March 3, 1931, Pete entrusted his newest lieutenant, undercover agent Lawrence Baldesareli, to take him to Omaha, Nebraska, to meet up with his *compari* to lay low and put some cash together.[105] Pete would pick up and deliver trunk loads of liquor in his car as he made his way east.

By March 1931, the Carlino gang was in disarray. Between the dozens of arrests, attorney fees, political payoffs and seizures of liquor, the Carlinos were running out of money. They were still unaware of the federal agent secretly planted in their midst. A plan was concocted to collect $11,500 on two separate insurance policies on Pete's Federal Boulevard home in Denver. Sam had successfully collected an insurance payout on his San Bernardino home when he firebombed it a year earlier.[106] Lawrence Baldesareli was present from the beginning stages of the planning to firebomb the Denver house. Just after midnight on March 17, 1931, Pete and Jennie's house at 3357 Federal Boulevard exploded as firebombs planted in three levels of the house demolished the two-story structure. No one was home at the

Headline of Pete Carlino's home being destroyed by a massive blast. *From the* Denver Post, *March 17, 1931, Denver Public Library.*

Top: Pete Carlino's house, 3357 Federal Boulevard, Denver, after bombs destroyed it on March 17, 1931. *Courtesy of Getty Images acquired from* Denver Post.

Bottom: Damage from the bombs that destroyed Pete Carlino's house, March 17, 1931. *Courtesy of Getty Images, acquired from* Denver Post.

time, and the press immediately assumed it was Pete's rivals enacting their vengeance.

Before he fled to Omaha, Pete had instructed them to contact Chris Murkuri, who was an authority on arson. Known as "Dynamite Chris," Murkuri was born in Albania and immigrated to the United States in 1912. The plan was to rig the house with enough accelerants to cover their tracks since it was going to be investigated. With the assassination attempt on

Pete one month earlier, he felt it would be easy to place blame on his rivals for the bombing. Unbeknownst to the Carlino brothers, Baldesareli had contacted the police and mayor's office through U.S. Attorney Ralph Carr and tipped them to the plot. The plan was to raze the house on March 14, but it was delayed. Police were aware that the blast was imminent but did nothing to prevent the explosion.

Baldesareli witnessed Sam and Pete discussing the plan with Joe Petralia, Pete's cousin, on March 2, 1931. Baldesareli stated that he returned on March 7, 1931, from dropping Pete off in Omaha and rejoined the gang when they were in discussions about the details of the job.[107] On March 12, the house was cleared of all the family heirlooms, and the contents were put into two trunks for safe keeping. The trunks were stored in the home of Joe Ferraro at 4785 Logan Street, Denver. Jennie had cousin Dan Colletti drive her to Pueblo. Sam gave Colletti the money to buy the materials for the job. Murkuri had given them a grocery list of ingredients that were required to complete the job.

On the night of March 14, Chris Murkuri and Carlino cousins Joe Petralia and Dan Colletti prepared the house for the explosion. Baseboards were removed so the liquid could penetrate every crevice, and devices were planted on both levels of the house as well as in the basement. Gasoline, turpentine, used motor oil and linseed oil completed the cocktail. Specified amounts were mixed to achieve the most productive effect. String was

Pete Carlino's home one year before the blast. Shown are Sammy Carlino, Chuck Carlino, Vic Carlino, Steve Carlino, Joe Carlino and Pete Carlino (sitting on stoop), with the Leonetti family (neighbors) in the background. *Courtesy of the Carlino family collection.*

intertwined with matches to create a delayed fuse that would allow the arsonists time for a clean getaway. The plan was to blow the house at midnight, but there was a delay. Leading up to the blast, the lights in the house had been turned on at sunset and off around 11:00 p.m. according to neighbors and a Denver police patrolman.

Just before midnight on March 16, 1931, Chris Murkuri, Joe Petralia and Dan Colletti lit the fuse and made their getaway. Joe Ferraro was waiting for them a few blocks away. The explosion was so immense it crumpled the house to its foundation. The blast was so severe that bricks were hurled blocks away and the entire roof was lifted and thrust toward the street. Neighboring houses had their windows blown out, and adjacent homes were damaged as well. The entire neighborhood was terrorized, as the shock waves were felt six blocks away.

The following day, local newspapers printed the motive as gang related and perpetrated by enemies of the Carlinos, while the police immediately suspected that it was an inside job. In fact, the police had known it was an inside job since March 2, when Baldesareli told U.S. Attorney Carr. Carr forwarded the information to Chief Reed and Mayor Stapleton, but there was no response. Shortly after 2:00 p.m. on Tuesday, March 17, police raided the home of Sam Carlino. Threatening to bust the door down, the police were greeted by Sam's wife, Josephine. A thorough search provided no new clues to the blast at Pete's house, and Sam was still at large.

The community was in an uproar that the current administration was doing so little to curb the bootleggers' activities.[108] There was a wave of public indignation directed at city hall, bringing attention to the fact that the police had been called several times regarding the Carlinos' associates blocking access in the alley to their properties while shipments of booze were being loaded and unloaded throughout the night.

Headline exposing the Denver Police Department's refusal to quell bootleg activities at Pete Carlino's house. *From the* Denver Post, *March 18, 1931, Denver Public Library.*

On March 19, police questioned Joe Petralia and Chris Murkuri for more than two hours regarding the blast.[109] They both denied any knowledge of who was responsible or why the blast occurred. Petralia was arrested later that day in connection with the explosion. The following day, the police learned of a tip provided by Lawrence Baldesareli regarding the location of the trunks containing the Carlinos' valuables. Hidden at the house of Joe Ferraro were the two trunks that held all of the Carlino heirlooms. After investigating the contents, the trunks were determined to be owned by the Carlinos.[110]

Police made a momentous discovery on Friday, March 20, 1931, when they stumbled across Sam Carlino and Lawrence Baldesareli by happenstance. One of the Denver Police Department's roving patrols saw two cars parked near the corner of Twelfth and Champa Streets. The first vehicle had two occupants displaying suspicious activities that made officers leery of their actions. Sam Carlino and Lawrence Baldesareli were arrested on the spot. After searching their vehicle, the officer discovered a slip of paper containing an address. The police investigated 1537 Marion Street and discovered a cache of hidden weapons. After his arrest, Sam told detectives that he knew he was wanted but was afraid to turn himself in because of the fear of being killed.[111] Sam told police that he suspected that his brother Pete had been killed because he had not heard from him in weeks.

The small arsenal contained 125 rounds of ammunition, a loaded automatic rifle, a loaded automatic shotgun and a loaded .22-caliber automatic pistol. Sam had been hiding out at an apartment on Downing Street, where a hat bearing his name was found.[112] When Sam was jailed, he discovered that Chris Murkuri, Joe Petralia and Dan Colletti had all been imprisoned with the same arson charges as he was. Joe Ferraro and Pete Carlino were named as suspects as well, but they were nowhere to be found. Newspaper reports suggested that Pete was in Chicago.

When Lawrence Baldesareli was arrested with Sam, he was only charged with carrying a concealed weapon (a minor offense). He was released upon paying a twenty-five-dollar fine.[113] The four members of the Carlino gang in jail contemplated their expeditious apprehension. They were curious how the police had rounded up precisely everyone involved in such short notice. Baldesareli's immediate release from jail cast doubt on his loyalty, and his confederates pointed a suspicious finger at him. With Sam Carlino and three of his henchmen jailed, Lawrence Baldesareli was now in charge of the Denver crew. Ironically, until Sam would be released from jail, an undercover federal agent was running the Carlino family bootlegging operation.

Above: Two trunks containing the valuables of Pete Carlino were found at cousin Joe Ferraro's house. Lawrence Baldesareli tipped the police where to find them. *From the* Denver Post, *March 20, 1931, Denver Public Library.*

Left: Trunks that were hiding Pete Carlino's heirlooms, found in the garage of Joe Ferraro after Lawrence Baldesareli tipped police to their whereabouts. These two trunks made the arduous journey to California after Jennie was given twenty-four hours' notice to leave Colorado. The trunks are in the possession of the Carlino family. *Courtesy of Michael Soo, photographer.*

Above, left: Sam Carlino mugshot. *Courtesy of the Carlino family collection.*

Above, right: Sam Carlino mugshot. *Courtesy Denver Police Department, Denver Public Library.*

Opposite, top: Political cartoon exposing Mayor Ben Stapleton and Police Chief Dick Reed's inability to cope with Denver's gangland activities. *From the* Denver Post, *March 21, 1931, Denver Public Library.*

Opposite, bottm: Headline announcing that Pete Carlino and five of his gang were charged with arson. *From the* Denver Post, *March 23, 1931, Denver Public Library.*

Sam was soon released from the city jail on a $5,000 bond furnished by Thomas Bettefratti, Guiseppe Cefalu and Mrs. Pietrina Vaccaro. Murkuri's release was effected when George Allison and Mrs. Victoria Hontos posted security valued in excess of $5,000.[114] Efforts to obtain sufficient security for the release of Colletti and Petralia failed, and their attorneys announced no further effort to obtain their freedom until after the additional filing of conspiracy charges.

By March 28, all four defendants had been bailed out. They were to be arraigned that Saturday. Court proceedings began at 10:00 a.m., but Sam, Joe and Dan were missing for their arraignment.[115] Judge Steele announced impatiently that if the three missing defendants did not show up by noon,

they would forfeit their bonds. At 11:30 a.m., the three men strolled in nonchalantly. Attorneys Earl Wingren, Charles Mahoney, F.E. Dickerson and T.J. Morrissey shouldered the blame and explained that they neglected to tell their clients the proper time. On Wednesday, April 1, 1931, Chris Murkuri filed for a separate trial, stating that he was innocent and was in no way related to the Carlino gang. Their trial was set for April 13, 1931.

AUTHOR'S PERSPECTIVE

When looking at the damage of Pete's house, it was evident they were dealing with a professional arsonist in Chris Murkuri. The massive amount of damage was isolated to the 3357 Federal Boulevard property. It is similar to the controlled demolition of buildings nowadays that bring down structures with explosives and leave the entire building within its footprint, limiting the damage to surrounding buildings. It is amazing to see the relatively restrained damage to the adjacent homes compared to Pete's house.

The disappearance of Ignazio Vaccaro, John Cha and his wife, Rose, plays into an interesting theory I have about them. I will discuss it in a later chapter. I remember asking my dad if it were true that Pete blew up his own house, and he responded, "Yes." I asked why, and he simply said, "He needed the money, they were broke." He was ashamed of what his father had done.

The two trunks that were found at Joe Ferraro's house containing the Carlinos valuables were the proof that the police needed to apprehend the Carlino gang. The trunks are still in possession of my family.

Chapter 13

"Più Strano di un Film Thriller"

Stranger than a Movie Thriller

On Saturday, April 11, 1931, Lawrence Baldesareli was on his way to pick up Sam at his house to bring him to a court appearance. He was living at the Mayflower Hotel on the corner of East Seventeenth Street and Grant. He had been driving Sam's car for the past month and walked to the private garage that was storing the vehicle.[116] When he returned to the Mayflower, he exited the car and was blasted with a shotgun as an old convertible Ford drove by with two men inside. Baldesareli was hit in the left arm and ducked for cover into the lobby of the Mayflower Hotel as a second shot was discharged. Several slugs of lead tore into his arm, and a few others took chunks out of the east wall of the hotel. He was carrying a .45 revolver but never had a chance to return fire.

Once he was safely inside the hotel, Baldesareli beckoned the hotel clerk, Robert Fuller, to contact his boss, U.S. Attorney Ralph Carr. Two good Samaritans, Charles Strong and C.F. Helmbecher, helped him into their car and drove Baldesareli to St. Joseph's Hospital. Police assigned two officers to stand guard at his room in case of another attempt on his life. Sam Carlino missed his court appearance when Baldesareli never picked him up. Police arrived at his house and arrested him and Jimmie Colletti. Sam had stated that he missed his court appearance because he was sick and could not get out of bed.

The press broke the news in the evening edition of the *Denver Post*. Details of Baldesareli's history with the Carlino gang were exposed, and the motive behind his attempted assassination was revealed. The *Denver*

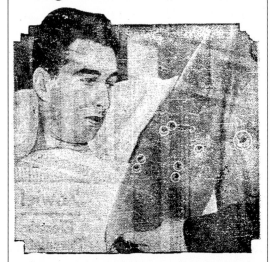

Above: Headline indicating the attempted murder of Lawrence Baldesareli. *From the* Denver Post, *April 11, 1931, Denver Public Library.*

Left: Lawrence Baldesareli showing reporters his jacket with multiple pellet holes from the shotgun blast that nearly killed him. *From the* Evening Tribune, *April 22, 1931.*

The uncovering of his undercover activities as an agent of the Federal Government resulted in Lawrence L. Baldesareli being put on the spot by gangsters at Denver, Col. Posing as a Chicago gunman, he wormed his way into the confidence of the most dangerous mob in town, and the work he did in this precarious position for six months helped to break up the gang. Baldesareli is shown in his hospital cot recovering from the effects of his "ride," and marveling at the havoc the leaden "moths" have wrought in his coat.

Post printed that he had been working with the Carlinos since August 1930 and had been assigned the duty as Sam's bodyguard. He spoke to the press and explained that he was assigned to find Dale Kearney's killer but was unsuccessful; he also detailed the dangers of being undercover and how his life was in jeopardy every day. He mentioned that gangsters were lousy shots and were only accurate when they used a shotgun.[117]

Ignazio Vaccaro had been missing since February 18, 1931, when he drove north from Trinidad toward Denver and stopped in Pueblo, where he was invited for dinner at a friend's house. This was the same time John Cha had been summoned to Denver. Police informants stated that after Vaccaro ate dinner, he was shot and killed and his body burned in the furnace of the homeowner. The identity of the host was never revealed.

On April 11, 1931, Carlino associate John Cha and his wife, Rose, were discovered living on a small orchard in Los Angeles after they disappeared with Ignazio Vaccaro in mid-February. Cha had been the main distributor of Carlino booze in Southern Colorado before he fled. When questioned why he left Colorado, he stated that he and his wife feared for their lives.[118] He expected that they would be killed if they remained involved with the Carlinos' bootlegging territories. The Chas had recently advertised their home for sale in North Denver, and a house they once owned in Trinidad exploded under suspicious circumstances. They would eventually move back to Trinidad after tensions subsided in the bootleggers' war. John's wife, Rose, was a crack shot with a gun. She was a champion skeet and trap shooter, as well as an avid hunter who was featured in many newspaper articles with her trophy kills. In 1938, John Cha would be convicted of embezzling public funds and serve a prison sentence. Cha eventually would become mayor of Trinidad in the early 1960s. He lived to the age of ninety-nine, dying in 1997.

Sam Carlino, Joe Petralia, Dan Colletti and Chris Murkuri were all re-arrested for the shooting of the agent. District Attorney Earl Wettengel asked the judge to raise their bond to $10,000 each.[119] Carlino attorneys vehemently objected. Wettengel also added Lawrence Baldesareli to the list of witnesses for the state. This drew another objection from Carlino attorneys, to no avail. Murkuri's request of a separate trial was denied. The Carlino gang suffered another blow when the trial date was rescheduled to May 6, 1931. It was delayed to allow Baldesareli time to recuperate. When the Carlino gang was ushered into court, they were flanked by six city detectives and a corps of federal agents. The feds had stepped up efforts to make sure that the Carlinos would not escape another conviction.

Police discovered that Sam Carlino had collected insurance money on a house fire that occurred at his San Bernardino home one year earlier.[120] The San Bernardino police chief wired Denver's Chief Reed and informed him that Sam Carlino had collected $5,200 the year prior. Sam's fire aroused no suspicion and was paid off immediately. The federal government took another step in shattering the Carlino organization by filing a charge of conspiracy to break Prohibition law on April 19, 1931. Joe Ferraro (Farrell) and Joe Borrello (Barry) were both arrested under the new charges.

Sam's situation was worsening every day. The brothers' plot to firebomb Pete's house backfired dramatically, a federal undercover agent

Sam Carlino and his attorney Frederick Dickerson. *Courtesy of the Carlino family collection.*

had busted up the gang, Pete was missing and on April 22, 1931, Sam was sued for $25,000 by car dealer Gilbert Stanley for an accident that had occurred a year earlier. According to Stanley, Sam was test driving an automobile in Happy Canyon when his reckless driving overturned the vehicle and caused him to be thrown from the car.[121] Stanley claimed that he suffered permanent injuries to his spine and had lost his sense of smell and taste.

If Gilbert Stanley wanted to collect his $25,000, he was going to have to wait a long time. On April 22, it was reported that Sam Carlino's attorneys quit after they realized he had no money to pay them.[122] F.E. Dickerson and T.J. Morrissey informed the judge that they would no longer be representing the Carlino group. The trial was set back again due to this new development. The new trial date was May 11, 1931.

AUTHOR'S PERSPECTIVE

Ignazio Vaccaro (Pete's bodyguard), John Cha and his wife were summoned to the aid of their boss, Pete, on February 18, 1931. They disappeared and were presumed dead. A rumor was circulated that Vaccaro was invited to a friend's house for a dinner and was killed and burned in a furnace. The police found his car with his revolver on the front seat near Colorado Springs but no signs of a struggle. Why would his car be left miles from Pueblo with the gun on the seat if he were killed at the house where he was visiting? When I discovered that John Cha and his wife turned up safe, I always wondered what happened to Vaccaro.

I have an interesting theory. Vaccaro was married to Pietrina (Aunt Pat). After Vaccaro's supposed death, Aunt Pat married Jennie Carlino's brother Charlie Riggio. She always held Jennie in contempt because she said that Jennie forced her to marry Uncle Charlie. I was just a young child when they both died, but hearing stories from my dad and older cousins makes me think that Vaccaro might have disappeared to get away from his nagging wife as much to get away from danger. According to my dad, his brothers and all of my older cousins, they claimed that Uncle Charlie was the kindest, sweetest person ever. Poor Uncle Charlie had to endure the wrath of this nagging woman for forty years. He would spend all day at the Time Market just so he would not have to hear her complain. I can see why Vaccaro would flee with Cha and his wife and escape to California. Why would the supposed killer of Vaccaro leave a valuable handgun on the seat of the car during the middle of the Depression? I believe that Vaccaro left it there to throw off the police and his boss.

Chapter 14

"*Salvatore*"

SAM

Joe Borrello had recently been wounded and survived, Ignazio Vaccaro was missing and presumed dead and a few weeks earlier, Carlino henchman Carlo Maurello was rubbed out in Pueblo. Pueblo police questioned Lena Mauro about Maurello's killing.[123] She was a housekeeper where Maurello was boarding, and ironically, she was the sister of Bruno Mauro. Bruno Mauro was a Carlino rumrunner and whiskey still operator. The enemies of the Carlino brothers were following the same playbook as when the Carlinos had plotted against the Dannas. Someone was systematically eliminating their bodyguards and associates to expose their real target.

Sam was released on bond on Wednesday, April 29, 1931.[124] His trial was less than two weeks away, and he was hidden in his house, fearful that he would catch an assassin's bullet. All of his firearms had been confiscated by the police, and he tried to keep a bodyguard with him at all times. The Colletti brothers, Pete's cousins Jimmie and Dan (real name Dominic), were assigned to protect Pete's wife, Jennie, and Sam. (Most are unaware that Jimmie and Dan were not blood brothers but rather were stepbrothers. Dan's father was Louis Colletti. Louis lost his wife, Margarita, to tuberculosis and remarried Josephine Amore. Josephine lost her husband in a carriage accident in Chicago, and she had a young boy named Jimmie Amore Jr. Once they were married, Jimmie was referred to as Jimmie Colletti.)

On the morning of May 8, 1931, Sam was at home with a crowded house full of guests. He lived at 3485 West Thirty-Third Avenue in Denver. Sam's wife, Josephine, was attending to their three-year-old daughter,

Jimmie and Dan Colletti (stepbrothers). *Courtesy of the Carlino family collection.*

Charlotte. Sam received a phone call from Bruno Mauro stating that he was in town visiting from Aguilar and wanted to stop by and say hello. When Mauro arrived, Dan Colletti greeted him. The three conversed for a few minutes until Jimmie Colletti entered with Jennie Carlino. Jimmie had noticed a man loitering outside Sam's house when they were arriving. When Jimmie Colletti entered the house, he shook Mauro's hand and greeted him. Bruno Mauro was a trusted member of the Carlino gang and had slept at Sam's house on several occasions, even sharing a bed with Jimmie and Dan Colletti. Jennie greeted Mauro and said, "I am surprised to see you, I heard you had jumped a federal liquor case bond and were a fugitive of justice." Bruno Mauro paid very little attention to what she was saying.[125] Sam's wife, Josephine, was still in her bathroom with her daughter, Charlotte, getting dressed to go downtown with her husband. Dan was to drive Jennie downtown to run some errands. As Jennie and Dan were leaving, he noticed the same suspicious character outside on the sidewalk whom Jimmie noticed. He wanted to confront the stranger, but Jennie dissuaded him. In her mind, there had been enough confrontation lately, and she didn't need another conflict for the family.

The three men talked in the family room for a few minutes and then said their goodbyes. Sam's last words to Mauro were "Goodbye friend." As Bruno Mauro opened the door to leave, he paused; at this time, Jimmie and Sam had started toward the kitchen when Sam turned back and yelled to Jimmie, "Look out." A shot rang out, hitting Sam in the back as he scrambled to the kitchen and collapsed. Bruno Mauro fired two more shots with a .45-caliber at Jimmie that missed. Mauro used a blue steel revolver loaded with slit-nosed bullets that were packed and boiled in garlic with the intention of making a poisonous round.[126] Jimmie tried to take cover behind a rocking chair as a third shot hit its target. Jimmie was shot in the abdomen.

Bruno Mauro fled the home and ran out the front door. Josephine saw him from their bedroom window running to an awaiting car behind the empty lot in the alley across the street between Thirty-Third and Moncrieff. The "lookout" man waiting in front of Sam's house accompanied Mauro to an awaiting black sedan as they sped off. The car was seen by a few witnesses, but no description of the shooter could be ascertained. Josephine ran to the kitchen and saw Jimmie Colletti standing over her husband as she shrieked. Most neighbors did not hear the gunshots that were fired but heard Josephine's mournful cries echoing throughout the neighborhood for several minutes. Sam was dead, and his lifeless body lay on the kitchen floor.

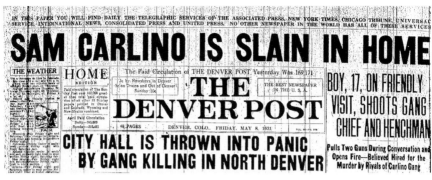

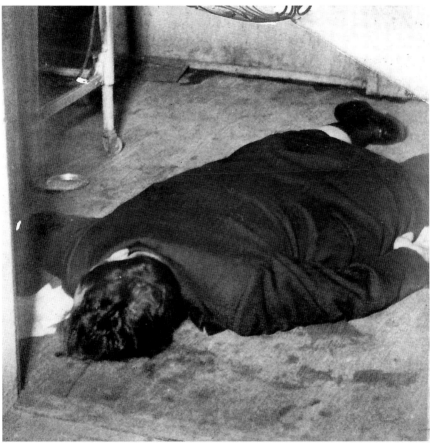

Top: Headline of Sam Carlino's murder. *From the* Denver Post, *May 8, 1931, Denver Public Library.*

Bottom: Sam Carlino shot dead, lying on kitchen floor. *Courtesy of the Carlino family collection.*

Jimmie Colletti mustered enough energy to run next door to alert a neighbor to call for help as Josephine tried to revive her listless husband. A neighbor, Mrs. J.B. Newman, arrived at the scene first and found Josephine sprawled over her dead husband's body trying to revive him. Josephine's face was smeared with blood, and three-year-old Charlotte stood by screaming.[127] Police arrived and questioned Josephine Carlino about who murdered Sam, and she blurted out hysterically, "Bruno Mauro, the same one who shot at Baldesareli."[128] She did not realize it at the time, but she had just broken the Sicilian code of silence in her state of grief. Josephine would not leave her husband's body, even as coroner's deputies tried to prepare him for the morgue. She screamed, "They can't take him, they can't take him, he's dead, the law ought to be satisfied now." Josephine was consoling her three-year-old daughter, Charlotte, when she told the police they had to pick up her four older children from school.[129] She begged them to bring them home because of fear that they would be targets as well. The police honored her request and escorted her four children home safely. Sam had been worried the last few weeks of his life that his children would also become targets.

Josephine was brought to police headquarters for questioning, and they showed her a photo of Bruno Mauro that she positively identified. On May 10, 1931, the newspapers reported that she had identified Mauro as the

Bruno Mauro's escape route leaving Sam Carlino's house after Sam's murder. Arrows show where Mauro ran to an awaiting car in the empty lot across the street. *Courtesy of the Carlino family collection.*

Pietrina Vaccaro, Josephine Carlino, Charlotte Carlino and Denver police detective William Clarke. *Courtesy of the Carlino family collection.*

shooter but also as the attempted assassin of Lawrence Baldesareli. Two days later, she would deny that she had stated that Mauro was the killer and rescind her statement that he was responsible for Baldesareli's shooting as well. Her family was at risk, and the stakes were high enough for her to keep quiet on who was behind the murder of her husband as well as the attempted murderer of a federal agent.

Jimmie Colletti had been rushed to Denver General Hospital and was followed by police detectives. The bullet that struck his abdomen had gone clean through, and after a few hours at the hospital, Denver district attorneys interviewed the wounded sixteen-year-old. Before he was interviewed, he asked police, "Did they get Danny too," referring to his stepbrother, Dan Colletti.

Deputy District Attorneys James T. Burke and Charles F. Morris questioned Colletti if he knew who the shooter was, and he denied knowing who shot him and who killed his boss, Sam Carlino. The district attorneys informed him that Josephine Carlino had identified Bruno Mauro as the killer and asked him the same question again. Once he heard that Josephine had broken the code of silence, he felt comfortable with telling the truth. He told the police how everything had happened.[130] During the police interview, members of the press were admitted inside Jimmie's room and allowed to ask him about the murder after he completed answering the district attorney's questions.

Before the press interview started, Colletti asked his nurse for a cigarette. The nurse said no, as the doctors were not sure if the bullet had passed through a lung, and they needed to see the results of the X-rays first. The *Rocky Mountain News* photographer wanted to take a photo of him, but he objected and gave the nurse an appealing glance.[131] She quickly grabbed a comb and ran it through his hair before the photo was taken. Colletti answered all of the reporter's questions about what happened and backed up Josephine's account of what had transpired. Jimmie Colletti initially kept silent about what occurred, but once he gave the same story as Josephine, the police were sure that Bruno Mauro was the killer.

Police Chief Reed contacted the surrounding cities of Colorado Springs, Pueblo, Trinidad, Aguilar and Cheyenne, Wyoming, to set up roadblocks to apprehend Mauro, but the efforts provided no results. Police raided the house of Bruno Mauro's brother, Pete Mauro, but failed to find any trace of him. Denver police also raided the rented house of Joe Roma and found nobody at home.[132] Roma was renting the house from Colonel Patrick J. Hamrock. (Hamrock was charged with murder, arson and larceny in his part of the Ludlow Massacre in 1914.)[133] A note left for the milk man to stop delivery until further notice was found on the porch. Lawrence Baldesareli had tipped them to check for Roma as the one who had planned the murder. Inside the house, they found a cache of weapons, including several shotguns, three rifles and boxes of ammunition for the guns.[134] Roma was being pursued by police as the mastermind behind the killing of Sam Carlino and the attempted murder of Lawrence Baldesareli.

Police had learned that an automobile that fit the description that Mauro escaped in was seen at Roma's rental house on Thursday one day before the murder. At Roma's home, police found two ledgers filled with cryptic notations in English and Italian and believed that they would be the key to cracking the gang's activities. Payments and receipts of nearly $3,000

Top: Jimmie Colletti in his hospital bed answering reporters' questions following the murder of Sam Carlino. *From the* Rocky Mountain News, *May 9, 1931, Denver Public Library.*

Bottom: Jimmie Colletti and Sam Carlino. *From the* Denver Post, *May 8, 1931, Denver Public Library.*

over a six-month period were discovered. Receipts for barrels, bottles and beet sugar in large quantities were found as well. The initials "I.V." were thought to be for Ignazio Vaccaro, who was still missing and presumed dead. Vaccaro was Pete's bodyguard as well as a lieutenant in the Carlino faction. Another set of initials found in the book read "P.C.G.," which possibly could indicate Pete Carlino Gang. Police admitted that other names existed but did not reveal them at the time.

The *Denver Post* had been exposing the ineptness of Denver police chief "Diamond Dick" Reed and Mayor Stapleton for their inability to quell the gangland violence that was terrorizing the city. Reed was nicknamed "Diamond Dick" for the enormous diamond ring he wore on his finger. In a May 10, 1931 interview, with elections less than two weeks away, Reed made the self-serving comment that he hoped to catch Sam Carlino's killer by election day. Reed then stepped into his luxurious Packard automobile and drove off. Reed's corruption far exceeded his ineptitude, as the *Denver Post* claimed.

Due to his intimate knowledge of the Carlino brothers' operation, Lawrence Baldesareli was advising the Denver police on who should be investigated. In an interview with the *Rocky Mountain News*, Baldesareli depicted the Carlino gang as fractured and its members as disloyal since the gang began its downward spiral starting in January 1931. "Some other faction bought off Bruno Mauro—if he is actually the man who did the job—and probably paid him or scared him into shooting Carlino. That's the way I figure it. Any member would sell out to a higher bidder," according to Baldesareli.[135] Mauro had a grudge with the Carlino brothers after he was instructed to take the fall for a whiskey still that belonged to Pete's cousin Joe Ferraro. He was promised that he would be compensated for accepting responsibility but was never paid because Sam was broke. Once word got out that the Carlinos were out of funds, their disgruntled crew were ripe for the picking by rival gang lords. Mauro was also suspected of the attempted murder of Lawrence Baldesareli in front of the Mayflower Hotel. Rumor stated that Mauro was owed $200 from the Carlinos.

Evidence surfaced in southwest Pueblo that the Ford touring car that was used in the attempted assassination of Baldesareli was found burning in a canyon. Ranchers saw the blaze and found the machine that had been dismantled. Sheriff Lewis Worker noticed that the license plate had not been destroyed in the fire and found that the car was sold to a Frank Sposito by Joe Roma's car lot. Frank Sposito was an alias Bruno Mauro had used in the past when he was caught moonshining (Mauro also used the alias Frank Asti at

Political cartoon depicting Mayor Ben Stapleton and Police Chief "Diamond Dick" Reed hiding under their desks in the wake of the Sam Carlino murder. *From the* Denver Post, *May 9, 1931, Denver Public Library.*

times).[136] The car was registered at 3054 West Thirty-Eighth Avenue Denver, home to Ignazio Vaccaro. Baldesareli identified the vehicle as the car that was driven during his assassination attempt, telling Chief Reed that he was certain it was the same machine used by the men who had wounded him in front of the Mayflower Hotel several weeks before. Roma had motivation to kill Sam

Headline indicating that Pete Carlino was recruiting "big-time" gunmen to help him overthrow Joe Roma in Denver, regardless of the cost of money or men. *From the* Denver Post, *May 10, 1931, Denver Public Library.*

Joe Bonanno stated the following regarding the national convention:[139]

> *It is important to underscore that the nature of this meeting was political. These men weren't coming together to sign contracts, or to form criminal cartels, or to organize illicit enterprises. Neither were these men going to Chicago as vassals paying tribute to their new master. It wasn't like that at all. The convention was held mainly to allow everyone to identify and place himself within the new political constellation of our world.*
>
> *The meeting itself was a showcase. The actual work had already been accomplished behind the scenes. Maranzano, for instance, had already been in contact with every major Father in our country. The only loose end in the national political picture was Chicago.*

The Pueblo-Denver area was important enough for the mafia to intercede in a problem between Scaglia's family and LaRocca in 1923 when Nicola Gentile was sent to mediate. Surely, Colorado was still relevant enough that Pete Carlino and Joe Roma would have been contacted by Maranzano about the Chicago convention. Pete's trip back east served three purposes. He pleaded his case to the head of the *Onorata Società*, avoided the assassins' bullets from his rivals in Denver and was lying low while he was waiting for the results of his arson trial. Newspaper reports on May 10, 1931, indicated that he was in Detroit, trying to put together a gang to take control of Denver. The *Post* reported that he was recruiting big-time gunmen to return with him to Denver to wipe out

120

Right: Pete Carlino sporting a mustache to conceal his identity since his disappearance on March 3, 1931. *Courtesy of the Carlino family collection.*

Below: Headline of U.S. Attorney Carr exposing Mayor Stapleton's foreknowledge of the bomb plot. *From the* Denver Post, *May 12, 1931, Denver Public Library.*

his enemies regardless of the cost of men and money. If this report were true, it certainly didn't help his chance of being crowned the "Boss of Colorado." This type of gangland violence was what the convention was aiming to cease. The senseless killings of rivals were making too many headlines and costing too many lives.

The Carlino arson trial began with startling testimony from U.S. Attorney Ralph Carr that put a dagger into the political hopes of Stapleton and Reed. Carr testified that these two men were to blame for the endangerment of lives when the Carlino blast occurred. Carr testified that they had known of the bomb plot five days before it occurred and knew the names of the men involved three days before the blast.[140] Chris Murkuri, Dan Colletti and Joe Petralia were only half of the men charged with arson. Pete Carlino and Joe Ferraro had disappeared, and Sam Carlino was dead.

WEDNESDAY, MAY 13, 1931 * THE DENVER POST—FIRST IN EVERYTHING THE POST PHONE—MAIN 2121 5

MAYOR STAPLETON, WHY DID YOU PERMIT ARSON BLAST?

6 THE POST PHONE—MAIN 2121 THE DENVER POST—FIRST IN EVERYTHING WEDNESDAY, MAY 13, 1931

STAPLETON AND REED ARE DENOUNCED IN OPEN COURT

News headlines denouncing Mayor Stapleton and Police Chief Reed in the Carlino arson case in open court. *From the* Denver Post, *May 13, 1931, Denver Public Library.*

The *Denver Post* had been the most outspoken of all the newspapers condemning Reed and Stapleton. In an open letter to the people, the *Post* printed a scathing accusation that Stapleton was in the back pocket of the bootleggers:[141]

> *Mayor Stapleton:*
> *What do you say to the sworn testimony of United States Attorney Ralph Carr that you knew all about the plot to blow up the Pete Carlino home?*
> *Carr testified in the west side district court Tuesday that he told you and your chief of police all the details of the plot FIVE DAYS BEFORE THE EXPLOSION OCCURRED and he testified he told your chief of police the names of the plotters THREE DAYS BEFORE THE EXPLOSION.*
> *Why didn't you do something to prevent the explosion? Why did you allow the gang conspirators to go ahead and destroy this property and endanger the lives and property of all the neighbors?*
> *How much more information do you have to prevent a crime than knowledge of when and how and by whom it is to be committed?*
> *You didn't even have to dig up the information about the plot to blow up the Carlino home. ALL THE FACTS WERE HANDED TO YOU ON A PLATTER AND THEN YOU DIDN'T EVER TURN A HAND TO PREVENT THE CRIME OF WHICH YOU HAD BEEN WARNED BY THE UNITED STATES DISTRICT ATTORNEY.*
> *IS THIS THE REASON YOU DID NOT INTERFERE WITH THE PLOT?*
> *Is it a fact Mayor Stapleton that you didn't interfere with or try to prevent the Carlino explosion because the Carlinos were trying to break in on the business of Denver bootleg gangs which had bought protection from someone in your administration?*

The accusation makes one wonder if Joe Roma had been tipped by the police that there was going to be a raid at the Bootleggers Convention in January. That could possibly explain why Roma and his two lieutenants (the

Smaldone brothers) were absent at the biggest gathering of bootleggers ever assembled in Denver.

After Carr's startling testimony, Lawrence Baldesareli took the stand and revealed all of the details of the Carlinos' operation. He detailed how the Carlino brothers were driven to desperation once their funds ran out.[142] He testified how he was constantly trying to talk Sam out of blowing up the house and how the blast date had been originally set for March 14, 1931. He described how a whiskey still on East Sixteenth Street, owned by the Carlino brothers, had been blown up and how the house of Carlino associate Joe Borello (Barry) had been raided and his guns taken from him, but no guns were taken from the Carlino opponents. The most stunning testimony Baldesareli gave was that he was promised by Pete an equal share of the Carlino brothers' bootlegging business if they were able to muscle in and take control of the Denver territory.[143]

Lawrence Baldesareli was the single most important reason the Carlino gang disintegrated. His tip to the police about the Bootleggers Convention and the evidence recovered in the Carlino family trunks after the explosion crippled the brothers' hopes of ruling Denver and most likely saved countless lives. He was the Donnie Brasco of his era. Just as Joe Pistone worked his way into the Bonanno family in 1976 and gained enough trust to be considered for membership, Lawrence Baldesareli had done the same thing forty-five years earlier.

There was quite a bit of political backlash after Carr's scathing testimony. On May 13, 1931, U.S. Attorney Ralph Carr outlined to the press the details of the correspondence he had with Lawrence Baldesareli leading up to the days of the explosion. He stated that the day of the blast he was out of town and instructed Baldesareli to try to talk Sam out of it. He instructed Assistant U.S. Attorney Ivor O. Wingren to notify police, but because it had been set so often and then delayed, he did not notify them again.[144] It made no difference because on Tuesday, May 19, 1931, Stapleton lost his bid for mayor.

The fates of Chris Murkuri, Dan Colletti and Joe Petralia were in the hands of the jury. According to a report in the *Denver Post*, Dan Colletti and

FATE OF CARLINO GANG IN HANDS OF JURY

From the Rocky Mountain News, *May 13, 1931, Denver Public Library.*

CARLINO BOMBERS GUILTY OF ARSON
Stapleton and Reed Denounced in Open Court

THE DENVER POST

THREE GANG HOODLUMS FACE 20-YEAR TERMS FOR BLOWING UP HOME

Above: Joe Petralia, Dan Colletti and Chris Murkuri were found guilty of arson in the Carlino blast. *From the* Denver Post, *May 13, 1931.*

Left: Sam Carlino. *Courtesy of the Carlino family collection.*

Joe Petralia were marked for death by the Roma faction. The two Carlino cousins were in quite a crisis.

On Wednesday, May 13, 1931, the jury found all three defendants guilty of the arson charges. The thirteenth juror was questioned after the trial and said that he would have voted for guilty as well. It was a major victory for the District Attorney's Office to finally win a crucial battle in its fight against gang violence in Colorado. The Carlino crew did get a break two days later when the government dismissed the pending liquor charges of conspiracy to violate national Prohibition laws.[145]

On May 18, 1931, Sam Carlino was laid to rest in a private ceremony at Crown Hill Cemetery in Wheat Ridge, Colorado. Sam was entombed there in the Tower of Memories in a plain pine coffin, surrounded by family and a handful of friends.

AUTHOR'S PERSPECTIVE

Pete's movements east were tracked by law enforcement tipped by Baldesareli. Perhaps Pete was trying to drum up support from other mafia figures in the more conservative cities such as Milwaukee in hopes of gaining their vote at the upcoming national convention being held in Chicago.

Pete's cousin Joe Petralia had just arrived from sunny Florida in December 1930. His hopes of making a fortune bootlegging with his cousin Pete backfired. He had been in Colorado for only four months, and he was in jail for arson and awaiting his verdict.

Chapter 16

"*Disappunto*"

CHAGRIN

Pete's journey east brought him face to face with Salvatore Maranzano, who had associates evaluate his situation back in Denver.[146] Pete's brother was dead, he was still wanted for arson charges and his crew had either been killed, imprisoned or betrayed him. His stock was falling among other leaders across the country, and he knew he had to return to his family and eventually capitulate. He was ordered to stay in New York until the mafia investigators had reported back to Maranzano with their findings.

By 1930, Carlino ally Paul Danna had moved to Brooklyn, New York, living in the same house (93 Truxton Street) as Salvatore Maranzano's brother Nicolo and nephew.[147] Paul Danna had been an alibi witness for Pete Carlino in 1926 for the murder of his cousins Tony and Pete Danna. Paul Danna had told police that Pete Carlino and John Mulay Jr. were playing cards with him in Aguilar just before the murders occurred in Pueblo.[148] It would be logical that Pete stayed with Paul Danna awaiting the verdict of the mafia investigation of his case back in Denver.

It is unclear whether Pete actually attended the national convention in Chicago in late May, but it is certain that he was in Milwaukee near the end of May 1931. Police testimony by Lucille Crupi placed Pete in Milwaukee at that time,[149] as noted in this excerpt from the book *Milwaukee Mafia* by Gavin Schmitt:

Milwaukee Police Report:
On Wednesday, June 3, 1931, Angelo LaMantia was handed over to federal authorities for deportation. He was wanted for a murder in Italy that occurred in 1926. Lucille Crupi, 30, Whiterock Avenue in Waukesha, was questioned by Captain H.C. Ridenour on Wednesday, June 3, 1931 at 3:35 pm. Crupi said she knew Frank and Vito Aiello, and she recalled when Isadore Aiello served time for dealing in whiskey. She said she had met Angelo LaMantia through her nephew, Frank LaGalbo. She also knew Pete LaMantia and identified a photo of him wearing glasses—though she said he no longer did and was now "very much fleshier." Crupi said her nephew, Frank LaGalbo went to Madison to meet someone who was in a dispute with him over alcohol and when LaGalbo approached his yard, the man shot LaGalbo in the foot. LaGalbo returned fire and shot the man in the stomach. Soon after, LaGalbo returned to Milwaukee and stayed at Lucille Crupi's apartment at the corner of 18th and Clybourn.

Crupi said that while LaGalbo was recovering, Angelo LaMantia and Jack Enea came up to see him. Enea had a bottle of booze. With them were Pete Carlino from Denver and a dark-haired man who was Carlino's partner. Carlino told Crupi, "they pinned a lot of murders on me, but can they prove it?" He handed Crupi a card with his name on it, said he was staying at the Martin, and offered to bring her back to Denver to meet his wife and kids where Crupi could be given a nice apartment and nice clothes. Carlino said the heat was on in Denver so he would have to hide out in Omaha for a while. He had intended to bring Jack Enea with him, but never followed through. Crupi said she had also seen Carlino in the Third Ward at Carl DiMaggio's restaurant, the LaTasca. She overheard Angelo LaMantia there talking to Carlino, Pete Guardalabene, Frank LaGalbo, Jack Enea and Vito Aiello saying they would have to leave at four in the morning to get a carload of booze. She overheard LaMantia talk on the phone in Italian to a man in Racine, saying they would pick up a full truck of booze and leave an empty truck there.[150]

Pete Carlino was meeting with the heads of the Milwaukee mob. He was planning to pick up a carload of booze, leave an empty truck and deliver the supply. While meeting Lucille Crupi, Pete's ego could not be checked, as he boasted about not being convicted for any murders. He had the audacity to invite Crupi to Denver to meet his wife and children and promised to set her up in an apartment and provide her with nice clothes. His wife, Jennie, and their six boys were living in squalid conditions back in

Denver, and he was making false promises of a pampered life in Colorado.

Pete had met with the *capo dei capi*, Salvatore Maranzano, in New York, and much to his chagrin, he was informed of his demotion. Maranzano was a "man of honor" in the *Onorata Società* and brokered a deal with Joe Roma to have Pete's life spared and put back on the friendly list. The respect and honor shared between two old-world gentlemen helped save him from certain doom.

Pete made the humbling journey west and arrived in Pueblo on Monday, June 15. He left his car at a repair garage in Bessemer, Colorado, owned by Joe Rotundo. He requested that Rotundo overhaul the motor. The car bore Wisconsin plates, and the identification numbers had been removed from the vehicle. His cousin Charles Guardamondo drove him to his farm five miles east of Pueblo. Pete's sons referred to him as "Uncle Charlie."

He was hiding out on the Guardamondo ranch when word got to his family that Pete was back in Colorado. Rumors stated

Pete Carlino after arrest in Pueblo. *Courtesy of the Carlino family collection.*

that gunmen were aware that Pete was back in town and that it would be a short time before he was discovered. Pete's sister-in-law, Catherine Mulay, was worried that killers would find Pete on the ranch and that the Guardamondo family would be in jeopardy. Catherine was Jennie's older sister and made the decision (unbeknownst to Jennie) to call the authorities and tip them to his whereabouts. Newspapers stated that Pete was turned in by friends, but it was actually his sister-in-law.

On Thursday evening, June 18, 1931, a coalition of police departments planned their capture of Colorado's most wanted man. Denver, Colorado Springs and Pueblo police descended on the Guardamondo ranch with a dozen officers armed with machine guns and sawed-off shotguns. Pete was standing outside when the cars pulled up to the property. He immediately ran into the house. The officers cleared the home of family members and gave an

Pete Carlino captured in Pueblo by twelve heavily armed police officers from Denver, Colorado Springs and Pueblo. *From the* Rocky Mountain News, *June 19, 1931.*

Pete Carlino captured and transported to jail in Denver. *From the* Denver Post, *June 19, 1931, Denver Public Library.*

order to Pete: "Give up or we will kill you." He was hiding upstairs before he walked obediently down the staircase and was immediately put into leg irons and manacles. Within minutes, a caravan of police cars was on its way to the Denver jail.

Police asked Pete how long he had been in town, and he replied, "A couple of days." They asked where he traveled to after he left Omaha, and he replied, "I'll tell it to the judge." When he was captured, he had only $42.50 in his pockets but was wearing a nice gray summer suit and an expensive handmade Panama hat. Pete was asleep and found snoring just ten minutes after he was put in his jail cell.

Jennie and her six boys were living in deplorable conditions in North Denver. Neighbors had to take a collection to help pay for their rent. Pete's son Sammy remembered stuffing cardboard in his shoes after the soles had worn through. The older boys were working odd jobs to help earn money, and seven-year-old Sammy would sell newspapers on Denver street corners to do his part. He learned to defend himself at an early age and would occasionally be challenged for the right to sell papers on a particular street. He would "win some and lose some," as he put it.

Immigration officer W.R. Mansfield met with Pete in his jail cell and discussed the possibility of dropping the charges of arson and deporting him back to Sicily. District Attorney Earl Wettengel agreed with the idea of deportation to save the expense of a trial. Pete listened politely but refused to answer any questions or discuss any details without the presence of his attorney.

Pete must have been pondering his epic rise and fall and what the future held in store for him and his family. The decision made in New York by Maranzano played a big part in Pete succumbing to his desire to exact revenge on his enemies. He understood that a decision had been passed down and he would have to abide by it or the penalty would be death (just as Nicola Gentile described in his book). He was a neutered leader with no gang to lead and was forced to reach out to the very person he once was allied with but now considered a rival. A call was made to Joe Roma to help him gain his freedom from jail. His bond needed to be posted and required a large amount of collateral to secure the bond.

Roma exhibited good faith in his agreement with Maranzano and made an extra effort to help Pete. Pete also reached out to family friends Guiseppe Cefalu and Caramella Cavalieri for their help to secure his bond as well. Properties owned by Cefalu, Cavalieri and Roma were used as the collateral to secure the $5,000 bond for Pete's release from jail.

Joe Roma posting bond for Pete Carlino's release. Roma was instructed by Salvatore Maranzano that Pete was to be shorn of power but not harmed. *From the* Denver Post, *Denver Public Library.*

Bond documents releasing Pete Carlino from jail. Properties of Joe Roma, Guiseppe Cefalu and Carmella Cavalieri were used as collateral to secure the bond. *Courtesy of the District Court of Colorado.*

On June 24, 1931, the *Rocky Mountain News* printed an article describing the secret conferences Pete had with Maranzano in New York and how he was stripped of his power and would be required to have a lesser role in the Colorado bootleg cartel. Authorities followed Pete and reported on his activities. The article mentioned his meeting with the leader of an international secret society, which we now know as the mafia.[151]

Following is the article published in the *Rocky Mountain News* on June 24, 1931:

GANG WARFARE IS ENDED HERE
PETE CARLINO RELEASED FROM JAIL ON BOND FROM "DEADLY ENEMY"
GANG WARFARE IN DENVER IS AT AN END!

Strong indication of the fact came yesterday when to the amazement of authorities, Pete Carlino deposed gang leader was released from County Jail on $5,000 bond posted by Joseph P. Roma, reputed to be his deadly rival. Carlino and Roma clasped each other by the arms. They shook hands. Roma signed Carlino's bond and Carlino called him "friend."

Bystanders gaped in wonder, but behind the scenes was another side of the story.

SECRET CONFERENCE
It was a tale of secret conferences, of negotiations between Carlino and the "boss" of an international secret society.

Roma, according to information obtained by authorities, has been given the society's scepter of power for Colorado.

Carlino, in consideration of gracefully accepting a position of less prominence than he formerly held, has been "put back on the friendly list."

Carlino, at that time was "out." A fugitive, his gang shattered, virtually broke, he was faced with the alternative of hiding the rest of his life or making peace on any terms.

He chose the latter course, Denver officials declared they learned.

MOVEMENT CHECKED
To New York, to Brooklyn, to the recognized leader of the secret society in America, Carlino made his furtive way—and his movements were checked by law enforcement officers.

Carlino placed details of his desperate situation before the society's chieftain. Authorities said he was told to remain in New York and wait word while the society's own representative checked the case.

Pete Carlino and Joe Roma outside the Denver Police Station answering reporters' questions after Roma posted his bond. *From the* Denver Post, *Denver Public Library.*

When their reports were turned in to "headquarters," a decision as to what Carlino should lose in the way of prestige and leadership was made.

His enemies were informed of the advantages to be gained by calling off the gang war.

Then, according to information in hands of authorities, orders were sent to Roma and others that Carlino was to be safe, but shorn of power.

Roma pledged property at 1919 Grant St. valued at $10,000 for Carlino's bond.

Always Good Friends
Other bondsmen included Guiseppe Cefalu, with $7,000 in property, and Caramella Cavaleri, with $10,000 worth of Jefferson county real estate. Dale Deane, assistant chief clerk of West side court, obtained an order from Judge Robert W. Steele to permit the Jefferson County property to be pledged.

"We have always been good friends" Roma said. "Sam Carlino was a good friend of mine too."

Sam Carlino was shot to death in his Denver home several weeks ago and search is still on for Bruno Mauro 17, who was named as the slayer.

Just as Nicola Gentile had been sent to evaluate and help mediate a dispute back in 1923 between Pellegrino Scaglia's family and Frank LaRocca, an assessor was sent to Denver to evaluate the Carlino-Roma dispute. Luckily for Pete, "old-school Sicilian" Salvatore Maranzano was making the decisions. At the national convention in Chicago, Maranzano declared himself the "Boss of Bosses," much to the chagrin of many other powerful mafia leaders. Tribute payments were provided at the Coney Island dinners held over several days in the summer of 1931. Al Capone gave him a gold watch and paid for the entire gathering at the Hotel Congress.[152] Maranzano's plan was to form a commission and allow the five families (Borgates) in New York to have a vote on how their families should be run. Unexpectedly, Maranzano announced at the Chicago meeting that he would be the *capo dei capi* (head of heads), and the attendees ended up with a dictator rather than a corporate governing body. He had also put together a list of his enemies who were to be removed to further his reach of power. The top name on his list was Salvatore "Lucky" Luciano.

The *Rocky Mountain News* article from June 24, 1931, is the missing piece of the Carlino puzzle. I can't believe that it sat stored away in my closet for eight years before I read it in its entirety. It verified Pete meeting with Maranzano and how Joe Roma was now the new ruling boss of Colorado. Roma was given specific instructions that Pete was to remain unharmed. As future events unfolded, it raised more questions about the Carlino-Roma relationship.

It was funny to read about how Pete was asleep just ten minutes after he was put in jail. My dad could fall asleep at stoplights while driving. Luckily, we diagnosed that he had sleep apnea, and he was issued a CPAP machine. When he was tested positive in his overnight test, they told him they could have his machine in a few days. He threatened to sleep there every night until he got one. They had one for him that very day.

Chapter 17

"Autostrada per l'Inferno"

HIGHWAY TO HELL

Pete's arson trial, originally set for July 14, 1931, had been set back to September 28. His accomplices were found guilty of the arson charges leveled against them, and Petralia and Murkuri awaited an appeal. Dan Colletti lied about his age and was given his sentence to be played out at the Buena Vista Reformatory instead of serving time at the Canon City prison. He said he was only nineteen, but the courts found records indicating he was actually twenty-two. Judge Robert W. Steele held that "he was a victim of circumstance and deserved a chance to make a man of himself."[153] On September 5, 1931, Chris Murkuri and Joe Petralia began their prison sentence in Canon City.

The political climate in New York was heating up as Maranzano began acting as a newly anointed king. "Lucky" Luciano, who helped him gain his throne, had heard through his contacts that Maranzano had plans to kill him and other members of the "liberal Americanized" wing of the mafia. Maranzano was rumored to have assigned the Luciano hit to Irishman Vincent "Mad Dog" Coll.[154] Luciano and Meyer Lansky put together a group of Jewish gangsters who were assigned to trick Maranzano into letting them into his well-guarded office at 230 Park Avenue, New York City.

Luciano had plans to reconfigure the hierarchy of the mafia and eliminate the dictatorship over which Maranzano ruled. Maranzano's conservative Sicilian influence on the *Onorata Società* in America was obsolete in the view of the younger and more broad-minded Luciano.

Luciano and partner in crime, Meyer Lansky, instituted a plan to eliminate Maranzano and three of his lieutenants in succession on the same day at different locations. This plan would be the inspiration for Mario Puzo in his depiction of Michael Corleone settling all his "family business" in one day in the climax of *The Godfather*.

According to Nicola Gentile, on September 10, 1931, an Italian and six Jewish gunmen recruited by Lansky entered Maranzano's Park Avenue office posing as federal officers and ordered his secretary, Grace Samuels, and the others to line up against the wall with their hands up.[155] Two of the fake agents covered the ten people in the outer office with guns as the others entered Maranzano's office and announced that they were federal agents. They ordered Maranzano's bodyguards to disarm and stand against the wall with their hands up. The Italian was called in to identify him and asked the men in the room, "Which one is Maranzano?" Maranzano turned and recognized a certain Peppino (Joseph) and replied, "Peppino you know I am Maranzano and that I am responsible for the office and that they can make any search they want because there is no contraband here....This office is clearly commercial." (Ironically, "Peppino" was Maranzano's pet name for Joe Bonanno.)

Maranzano, having been positively identified, was brought into an adjoining office and stabbed six times. He fought back ferociously, and when he would not succumb to his attackers, he was shot four times until he died. The gunmen escaped, and the next phase of the *coup d'etat* was set in motion.

Later that day in New York City, Luciano's hitmen located Vincenzo (Jimmy Marino) LePore, who was a Maranzano lieutenant and sympathizer. He accompanied his two daughters to get a haircut and was shot while standing in the doorway of the barbershop. A car drove up and blasted him before fleeing the scene. Sam Monaco and Louis Russo were Maranzano's trusted underlings and were captured, beaten and tortured before they were killed and their bodies thrown in the Hackensack River in New Jersey. Their decomposing corpses would be found days later on September 13, 1931, in New Jersey.[156] Luciano had given the order to eliminate Maranzano sympathizers.

According to legend, Luciano killed more than forty Maranzano sympathizers on September 10, 1931. In the book *The Valachi Papers*, Joe Valachi recounted the Bo Weinberg story of the "night of the Sicilian vespers" in which there had been a great purge of mafia leaders across the country.[157] After the *Valachi Papers* laid out the story, other authors took Valachi's word as gospel and did not fact-check to see if his story was actually accurate. Other authors would add to the count throughout the years until it had reached a number as high as ninety.[158]

Before 1976, Humbert S. Nelli (professor of history at the University of Kentucky) traveled to fifteen cities in the United States in his pursuit to document the history of the mafia in the United States.[159] Before there was access to enormous databases online, Nelli had to travel to each of the major mafia cities to do his research. Nelli found only four murders other than Maranzano's that occurred on September 10, 1931, across the entire country that could have been related to the Maranzano *coup d'etat*. Three were in the New York/New Jersey area with the slaying of LePore, Monaco and Russo, and one was in Colorado. (Until now a link had never been established.)

Pete Carlino was living with his family in North Denver under impoverished conditions. His arson trial was nearly two weeks away, and he made plans to visit his two associates, Chris Murkuri and Joe Petralia, at the Canon City Penitentiary. He departed Denver on Wednesday, September 9, and headed to Pueblo to stay overnight at his cousin Charlie Guardamondo's house. He arrived nearly at midnight and was up early to leave the Guardamondo ranch by 6:30 a.m. He had been in contact with Joe Petralia and confirmed that he would be arriving at the prison on Thursday, September 10.

Charlie Guardamondo. *Courtesy of the Carlino family collection.*

While traveling to the prison in Canon City, Pete's Dodge coupe (no. 73-926) was forced off the road by two cars and ran into a ditch. His Dodge was hidden in a clump of bushes two miles west of Penrose. While traveling through Wetmore, Colorado, on Thursday morning, several witnesses saw Pete accompanied by three men followed by a second car also containing three men.[160] He was driven about twelve miles away to remote Siloam Road, where he was shot twice in the back and once in the head at close range. The slugs that entered his back traveled completely through his rotund frame. The shot to his head was so violent that it tore away a significant portion of his skull and left him almost unrecognizable. His body had fallen next to a small bridge

Top: Pete Carlino's decomposing body was found three days after his disappearance on his way to visit Joe Petralia at the Canon City State Penitentiary. *From the* Denver Post, *September 14, 1931, Denver Public Library.*

Bottom: Pete Carlino was found dead, shot three times on Siloam Road outside Pueblo. *From the* Rocky Mountain News, *September 14, 1931.*

that was adjacent to an arroyo. For two days, his body lay undiscovered until it was moved next to the roadside sometime between Saturday night and Sunday morning.

On Saturday evening, two phone calls were placed regarding the murder of Pete Carlino. Jennie received a call in Denver from an unrecognizable voice stating, "You had better start for Pueblo at once, something has happened to your husband." She replied, "Where is Pete?" and the caller hung up. She immediately made for the Denver police station to inform them of the call.[161]

At about the same time, a call was placed to Pueblo police telling them where to find the body. The call was untraceable, and the anonymous caller hung up. Coroner C.N. Caldwell of Pueblo County and his deputy, Pete Coe, found the body of Pete Carlino and determined that he had been moved recently from near the bridge to the side of the road. Letters in his pockets identified him, as did the signet ring he wore. Captain Rube E. Pratt and Detective W.L. McDonald positively identified the body to be Pete Carlino, as they knew him personally.[162] Fingerprints matching Pete were the final confirmation. The coroner stated that the killers employed poisonous bullets similar to what had been used on Sam Carlino and Jimmie Colletti. After examination of the body, the coroner discovered that the fleshy areas around the wounds were badly discolored, indicating the poisonous infection had set in.[163]

Jenny was too afraid to go to Pueblo to identify her husband and had arrangements for Pete to be brought to Denver. She stated to police that she and her six boys would remain in hiding until the funeral. On Tuesday, September 15, 1931, Pete Carlino's funeral consisted of a short prayer by Father Giglio (he baptized Pete's son Joe in 1916) in Pueblo before the body was brought by hearse to their ramshackle rental house at 2523 Eighteenth Street in Denver. His casket was simple, not because of lack of vanity but because Jennie had no money to afford the funeral and the money had to be borrowed by friends. The private gathering consisted of family members, friends and a half dozen of his former associates. Dusk was approaching, and inquisitive neighbors stood on their porches to see the infamous Pete roll by on his final ride home.

Pete's sons—Vic, Joe, Chuck, Steve, Sammy and Pete Jr.—stood outside the hearse in a line, all dressed in new matching black suits, black shirts and black ties. A voice was heard, "Just leave him out here—don't bring him inside."[164] Pete's body remained in the hearse as the family gathered in the living room of the house. Jennie, who had been veiled for hours, sat weeping, as no one spoke. Jennie then broke the silence, as featured in the *Rocky Mountain News* on September 16, 1931:

> *"Are they going to say the nasty things—the awful things they have been saying?" Without waiting for an answer she continued, "Good Father and Husband." "Gangs, gangs, gangs—that's what they keep saying about him—about Pete. How do they know he was gangs? Nobody ever saw him kill people—nobody can say they know he was gangs. He was a good Father—a good Husband, he was good to everybody but they say mean*

nasty things about him. They have made me suffer—me, my children about me and him always such a good father."

Jennie's grief was accompanied by a dose of denial.

The family proceeded outside to escort the body to the cemetery. Pete's older sons cleared the street as passing motorists were stopping out of curiosity. "Ma don't want you standing out here," the boys challenged. Perhaps it was the magic of the once powerful Carlino name, or it may have been a natural sympathy for all the family of the dead. All obeyed, and the street cleared as the little procession moved on. Pete Carlino was placed in the mausoleum next to his brother Sam at Crown Hill Cemetery.

Investigators never discovered who killed Pete, but Pete Carlino's sons knew who had him set him up to be killed. Cousin Joe Petralia had orchestrated the meeting with Pete at the Colorado State Penitentiary in Canon City, Colorado, on September 10, 1931. Petralia was disgruntled with serving a six- to ten-year sentence, and his animosity toward Pete was discovered. Joe Roma learned of his antipathy toward his cousin and used that as his way to trap Pete on a secluded highway outside Pueblo.

Rudy Constantino, Sam Carlino, a man who could be Raffaele Smaldone and Joe Petralia, Denver, 1931. *Courtesy of Peter Carlino III.*

Joe Petralia, Dan Riggio, a man who could be Raffaele Smaldone, Sam Carlino and Rudy Constantino, Denver, 1931. *Courtesy of the Carlino family collection.*

Did Lucky Luciano contact Roma and give the go-ahead for him to push the button on his old rival, or did Maranzano give the order to Roma to eliminate Carlino? Was the date of his death occurring at the same time as other Maranzano sympathizers just a coincidence?

One fact is certain: when Roma was shot dead two years later in his home by trusted friends, three letters from Joe Petralia were found in his pocket.[165] The first two sent to Roma were friendly in nature, asking for a favor (evidently Roma demurred), and the third was scathing and threatening. Why would Joe Petralia, a Carlino family member and convicted arsonist, ask the head of the Colorado Mafia for a favor—while in prison—if he had not done something considerable to earn it?

AUTHOR'S PERSPECTIVE

I feel the decision to murder Pete was carried out at the highest level. He was a victim of his insubordinate behavior. He allowed a federal agent into their family. He also allowed the purpose of his trip back east to be showcased in the June 24 newspaper article. These two factors must have played a major role in the decision to kill him.

Dominick "Sonny Black" Napolitano was executed in 1981 for allowing FBI undercover agent Joe Pistone (Donnie Brasco) into the Bonanno family. It would not have been a surprise that Pete had been executed for the same reason fifty years earlier.

It is interesting that Nicola Gentile mentioned that Maranzano used the name "Peppino" (Joseph) when speaking to the Italian man when questioned. Gentile also used parentheses around the name "Joseph" in his book. Theories abound whether Joe Bonanno aided the Luciano-Lansky killers in Maranzano's office by identifying him. Bonanno denied that he was part of the plot to kill his boss, but logic would say that he probably was. Bonanno was twenty-six years old and was offered the opportunity to be the boss. He knew that if he sided with the old man, he would be on Luciano's kill list as well. Self-preservation is a powerful motivator.

Chapter 18

"Il Fuorilegge Josie Carlino"

The Outlaw Josie Carlino

Josephine Carlino was in fear for her life, as well as the lives of her five children. She escaped to San Diego, California, in August 1931 to be close to her aging mother and her father, Phil Piscopo.[166] Her sister Anna Danna, widow to Pete Danna, had moved to San Diego years earlier with her children following her husband's murder. The two families were close despite their husbands' bloody history. Years later, Thanksgiving and Christmas would be shared, and no mention of their past in Colorado was ever spoken of again.

Jennie and her six boys were struggling to cope with the loss of their family patriarch. For all the bad that Pete had done in his life, he has to be credited with instilling a sense of honor, love of family and a hard work ethic in his sons. Those are character traits that the Carlino boys would display during their life and would be passed on to the next generation of Carlinos. His sons resented him for not being prepared for such a calamity as being murdered. He carried no life insurance policies that would have guaranteed his family a chance to maintain a home during the Great Depression. The two insurance policies he did have were for the house that he purposely destroyed.

In January 1932, foreclosure proceedings began against Jennie for nonpayment of $4,000 for the house on Federal Boulevard in Denver that was leveled in the blast. The foreclosure was instituted by Pasquale and Josephine Muro, who held the note on the home. Jennie's problems were amplified when the Potomac Insurance Company and the Homestead Fire Insurance Company refused to pay the settlement on the Federal Boulevard property

Joe Carlino, Pete's second-oldest son. *Courtesy of the Carlino family collection.*

because they claimed that Jennie was a part of the plan to defraud them. Jennie petitioned the court to sue the two insurance companies for $5,750 each and was granted that right at the county's expense. Judge George F. Dunklee approved the suit, as the proceeds would be prorated between her and the Muro couple if she were to be awarded a judgment.

The Great Depression was taking its toll on the country, and the Carlino boys were desperate to help provide for their family. Fifteen-year-old son Joe Carlino would quit high school and resort to bare-knuckle brawls to earn extra money for his mother. Unsanctioned, illegal street matches were common in that era, and Joe Carlino would put the welfare of his body on the line at every match.

Sixteen-year-old brother Vic would be the bookie for his younger brother's matches, taking bets and making odds. Joe recalled almost being beaten to death by a man nicknamed "Crow." Joe and his younger brother Chuck would have successful local boxing careers in San Jose, California, up to the start of World War II. They both fought under the name Carlin, instead of Carlino, because it was difficult for Italians to get matches at the time.

On February 24, 1932, Bruno Mauro was accompanied by attorney Charles T. Mahoney when he surrendered to Denver police for the murder of Sam Carlino. D.A. Wettengel stated that first-degree murder charges would be filed in the West Side Criminal Court.[167] Mauro had been on the lam for ten months and told police that he had been living on a ranch in Southern Colorado. He stated that he read the newspapers and saw that he was wanted for murder and wanted to turn himself in. He claimed that he hitch-hiked from Pueblo to Denver and went to Mahoney's office to facilitate his surrender. Mauro also claimed that he was in Southern Colorado at the time of Sam Carlino's murder.

The police admitted that Jimmie Colletti (the only eyewitness to the murder) could not be located. Their other witness, Josephine Carlino, had

Jennie Carlino. *Courtesy of the Carlino family collection.*

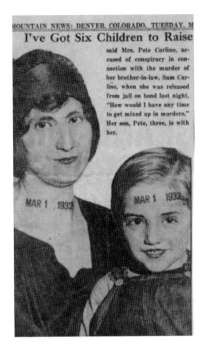

MOUNTAIN NEWS: DENVER, COLORADO, TUESDAY, M

I've Got Six Children to Raise

said Mrs. Pete Carlino, accused of conspiracy in connection with the murder of her brother-in-law, Sam Carlino, when she was released from jail on bond last night, "How would I have any time to get mixed up in murders." Her son, Pete, three, is with her.

MAR 1 1932   MAR 1 1932

Jennie Carlino and son Pete Jr. *From the Rocky Mountain News, March 1, 1932, Denver Public Library.*

only seen Mauro running from the house and rescinded her stated version of the events to the police. Twenty-five witnesses (mostly police officers) were placed on the witness list, as well as Jimmie Colletti and Josephine Carlino. Wettengel stated that without the testimony from Colletti and Carlino, the state would have a hard time prosecuting the case. Wettengel tried to induce Josephine Carlino to return to Denver from San Diego to testify in the trial, to no avail.

On February 27, 1931, District Attorney Earl Wettengel made a desperate move and arrested Pete Carlino's widow, Jennie, for conspiracy to commit murder and accessory after the fact for the slaying of her brother-in-law, Sam Carlino. She was accompanied by her three-year-old son, Pete Jr. Denver police chief Clark orchestrated the arrest of Josephine Carlino in San Diego for the same charges. Although extradition between California and Colorado was not common, Wettengel appealed to Governor James Rolph of California for the extradition to be approved. "Maybe these people won't be so reluctant to talk when they see the penitentiary staring them in the face," said Chief Clark. "We're going to take them all into court and see if we can't break down this silent alibi which has been built up for Mauro."

The Denver police arrested Joe Roma at his grocery store at 3420 Quivas Street in Denver. Roma was sitting in the sunshine in front of his store when investigators Ray Humphreys and Stanley Maus approached him.[168] After exchanging greetings, they informed Roma that they had to take him in. He said, "Okeh." "Do you have a rod [revolver]?" asked Humphreys. "No—no gun," responded Roma. A search of him substantiated his assertion. Roma posed for photographers after his arrest and joked to a *Denver Post* reporter, "Don't make the story too rough....I don't like to have you give me big headlines." Luckily for Roma, the headlines were kept to a minimum, because the biggest news story across the country was the kidnapping of Charles Lindbergh's baby.

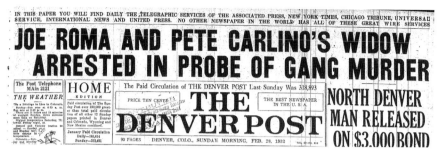

IN THIS PAPER YOU WILL FIND DAILY THE TELEGRAPHIC SERVICES OF THE ASSOCIATED PRESS, NEW YORK TIMES, CHICAGO TRIBUNE, UNIVERSAL SERVICE, INTERNATIONAL NEWS AND UNITED PRESS. NO OTHER NEWSPAPER IN THE WORLD HAS ALL OF THESE GREAT WIRE SERVICES

JOE ROMA AND PETE CARLINO'S WIDOW ARRESTED IN PROBE OF GANG MURDER

THE DENVER POST

NORTH DENVER MAN RELEASED ON $3,000 BOND

DENVER, COLO., SUNDAY MORNING, FEB. 28, 1932

Above: Joe Roma and Jennie Carlino were arrested for conspiracy to commit murder and accessory after the fact. *From the* Denver Post, *February 28, 1932, Denver Public Library.*

Left: Joe Roma posing for photographers outside the Denver Police Station, 1932. *Courtesy of the Carlino family collection.*

Opposite: Jenni Carlino's mugshot. *Courtesy of the Carlino family collection.*

Roma was initially ordered to be held incommunicado but was later permitted to be counseled by his attorney, Arthur Morrison. Judge McDonough set his bond at $3,000, and Roma's wife, Nettie, made the arrangements for his release.

San Diego police chief H.H. Scott informed Denver's Chief Clark that Josephine Carlino would fight extradition. "If they get me back to Denver they will have to do some fighting," stated Josephine.[169] Denver police grilled Jennie Carlino for three hours, but she refused to repeat her previous statements to police. The prosecutors were banking on the threat of jail as a motivator for the Carlino widows to testify, but they underestimated the power the *Onorata Società* had as a threat to the widows' families. Both Carlino widows understood that the real threat was from Joe Roma, not from serving jail sentences.

Colorado governor Billy Adams appealed to California governor Rolph to extradite Josephine Carlino back to Denver. For the first time ever, motion pictures filmed at the crime scene and at the autopsy were used to influence an extradition. More than two hundred feet of film was shot of the crime scene, surrounding areas of the Carlino home and the escape route, as well as the autopsy. The film depicted Deputy Coroner George H. Bostwick examining Sam's body at the morgue and showed the point of entrance and exit of the bullet.[170] The movie was shown to California governor Rolph to help persuade him to sign the extradition papers. Josephine, held at the San Diego jail since her arrest, was ordered by Governor Rolph to return to Denver to testify in the Bruno Mauro case.

Policewoman Edith Barker and Deputy District Attorney James T. Burke departed Colorado en route to San Diego to escort Josephine Carlino back to Denver to testify. Wettengel made a statement about the case and responded, "People can't be near the man when he is shot and around the body afterward, make statements [about] the identity of the killer and later, when he is captured, change their stories around to acquit the man….Gangster or no gangster, Carlino's life was taken and I mean to get every bit of the truth available about the murder."[171]

The Carlino widows were not the only ones feeling the heat in the run-up to the Mauro trial. District Attorney Earl Wettengel and his staff were receiving death threats regarding the trial of the Sam Carlino murder.[172] The pressure being levied against Joe Roma had led to these threats against Wettengel. Police were still looking for Dan and Jimmie Colletti, who saw Mauro at the Carlino house just before the murder. Dan Colletti served a short term at the reformatory and had been released in December 1931 for his part in the Carlino bomb plot that destroyed Pete Carlino's house. Jimmie Colletti was still missing and presumed to be in New Jersey.

Jennie's second-oldest son, Joe, waited all day at the West Side courthouse until Joe Roma had facilitated her release. Two days after her arrest, Jennie Carlino and her three-year-old son, Pete Jr., were released on bond, which had been arranged by Joe Roma. Roma had particular interest in making

Josephine Carlino in Denver after her extradition from San Diego. Policewoman Edith Barker is in background. *Courtesy of the Carlino family collection.*

sure that the Carlino widows would remember to swear an oath of amnesia before swearing their oath to tell the truth.

Just days after Joe Roma had been bailed out of jail, he arranged for Jennie Carlino's release. Roma was surprised when he was arrested again as he was indicted for the attempted murder of Lawrence Baldesareli. Just as before, police found Roma at his Quivas Street grocery store, this time sitting inside at a table with Max Wine, Clyde Smaldone and another

The Paid Circulation of THE DENVER POST Yesterday Was 317,153

3c by Newsboys in Denver
5c on Trains and Out of Denver
Sundays 10c

THE DENVER POST

Denver Post Paid Circulation for January.
Daily—185,614
Sunday—313,491
The Best Newspaper in the U. S. A.

HOME EDITION

DENVER, COLO., MONDAY, FEB. 29, 1932.

24 PAGES
VOL. 40—NO. 244.

WETTENGEL RECEIVES DEATH THREATS IN CARLINO PROBE

ROMA CALLED BEFORE COUNTY GRAND JURORS

Pastor Who Says He Has Been Threatened Also Will Testify.

In the face of mysterious death threats and sinister warnings to "lay off" Denver gangland, District Attorney Earl Wettengel was reported to be all set Monday to "blow the lid off" he underworld" and wage a fight to a finish to bring to justice gunmen responsible for recent killings, including the slaying of Sam Carlino, North Denver racketeer.

Threats against Wettengel and his special investigators, Ray Humphreys and Stanley Maus, followed he filing of complaints charging conspiracy and accessory in the Carlino murder case against four persons.

Death Threats against the district attorney and two of his special investigators as a result of their activity against gangsters created an atmosphere of tenseness around the west side court, Monday. The trio are shown below.

STANLEY MAUS.   EARL WETTENGEL.   RAY HUMPHREYS.

There were death threats against Earl Wettengel and his staff during their probe of Sam Carlino's murder. *From the* Denver Post, *February 29, 1932, Denver Public Library.*

unidentified man eating a fish dinner. "Wettengel wants to see you," said the deputy. "Okeh," Roma responded. "I'll be right with you." A revolver lay next to each man's plate at the table.[173] He emptied out his pockets, and several revolver cartridges were placed on the table. "Take care of these," he instructed Smaldone. A grand jury found that he had participated in the attempted slaying of undercover federal agent Lawrence Baldesareli in April 1931. A $50,000 bond was required for Roma's release. Grand jury investigators delved into Roma's bank accounts and received information on his gangland activities. Later that afternoon, Roma was released when more than $300,000 worth of property was secured to facilitate his $50,000 bond.

Josephine Carlino was making her way back to Denver, flanked by two Denver enforcement officers. They must have convinced her on the train ride east to tell the truth about the events on May 8, 1931, because when she arrived in Denver, she announced that she would testify that Bruno Mauro was the man who shot and killed her husband.

Once she arrived, Josephine Carlino was booked and charged with accessory to murder in the death of her husband. She stated to police that the story she told at the time of the murder was the correct version and expressed a willingness to repeat that story to a jury regardless of the consequences to her. "They'll kill me, but I don't care," she asserted.

Jennie Carlino, Mrs. Vaccaro (Ignazio's mother) and Pete Carlino Jr. *Courtesy of the Carlino family collection.*

SAM CARLINO WIDOW AGREES TO TELL TRUTH OF HIS DEATH

Josephine Carlino agreed to testify against Bruno Mauro. *From the* Denver Post, *March 15, 1932, Denver Public Library.*

"They'll kill me like a yellow dog." Officers who accompanied her from San Diego said that she was in a veritable torment of fear. Deputy D.A. Burke wired to Wettengel to have additional police protection from the trip from Trinidad to Denver as they passed through those cities.[174] Details of police guarded the train at Pueblo and Trinidad, and the party was met at the Denver station by a squad of officers.[175]

Josephine announced that she would make no effort to raise the $10,000 bond that was set for her release. "I might be better off here," she stated, "I don't believe I could raise the bond if I wanted to get out of jail." Burke added that she made a significant statement on the train to him when she said, "Bruno Mauro would not have dared kill my husband if he had been facing him."

Shortly after she was admitted to jail, Josephine conferred with attorney Arthur Morrison, who obtained an order from Judge Steele to see her. Morrison said he was engaged by friends of Josephine to represent her on her criminal charges. What Josephine did not know at the time of her meeting with him was that Joe Roma had hired Morrison to silence her testimony to his favor.

Morrison's chicanery did not go unnoticed, as Earl Wettengel learned of the plot to enlist Roma's "chosen" attorney to represent Josephine; Wettengel informed her that she was not obligated to have representation and did not need to talk to anybody against her will. Wettengel stated that the purpose of Arthur Morrison's visits were to persuade her not to tell everything she knew. "Mrs. Carlino wants no counsel," Wettengel said. "Despite her attitude this lawyer called on her after she told him she wanted no representation in court. I have been informed that Mrs. Carlino was approached to withhold information in the Mauro case. She is afraid to be out of the County jail because she is apprehensive of her safety. The woman has told me that she believes an effort may be made to take her life if she tells everything she knows about the murder of her husband."

Fearful that "outside influences" would persuade Mrs. Carlino, Wettengel filed a petition with Judge Frank McDonough Sr. to have a deposition taken from her. Mauro attorney Charles T. Mahoney was notified, and Wettengel

Detective George Farrar, Detective Bert Kistler, Josephine Carlino and Deputy Sheriff Arthur Massie at Crown Hill Cemetery. *Courtesy of the Carlino family collection.*

Josephine Carlino and Ray Humphreys walking to the Denver Courthouse on March 20, 1932.
Courtesy of the Carlino family collection.

indicated that the charges of accessory to murder would be dropped, and after her deposition, Josephine Carlino could return to her home in San Diego. Mahoney objected to the deposition planned for Saturday, March 19, but it was overruled.

Josephine petitioned the court to visit her husband Sam Carlino's grave and was granted the unusual request by Judge Robert W. Steele. It was a brilliant strategy to let Josephine visit her husband before she was to give her deposition. On Friday, March 18, 1932, police guards escorted her to the Tower of Memories to visit Sam one last time. Once inside the mausoleum, she was overtaken by grief and screamed, "I'll get even," the words echoing around the hallowed walls. While viewing Sam's crypt, she became hysterical and had to be escorted from the mausoleum.

The following day, Josephine arrived with Ray Humphries to the courthouse. She had survived any plans that might have been made to quell her testimony. She gave her account as she had that last May, how it really happened, but made two subtle changes that might have gotten her off the hook with Roma. When asked if she had looked outside, she said "yes." Then she was asked, "Whom did you see?" Her reply was, "Nobody at first." Then she was asked about when she entered the kitchen and what she had heard from her husband and Jimmie, and she replied, "My husband was dead, he could say nothing, I said to Jimmie *that he killed him*, and he told me it was Bruno Mauro that killed him....I didn't see the shooting." Then she was asked about what she had seen outside again, and she mentioned a man walking back and forth in front of the house. She was asked, "Was this Bruno Mauro?" and her reply was, "No." Without Jimmie Colletti's testimony, the prosecution's hopes for the case were dwindling.

Josephine was escorted back to the jail and spent her last evening in Denver. As promised, she was heading back home to her family in San Diego. Ray Humphreys called her out of her cell at 3:30 p.m., as she was already packed and dressed for her trip. The police took every precaution to smuggle her in secret to Union Station to catch the 4:00 p.m. train out of town. She had a smile on her face and told Humphreys, "I want to go back to my *kiddies*....I am so glad, but I am so worried too." She added, "I am afraid of what might happen to me over what I told of my husband's murder." The police escorted her onto her Pullman car through the railroad yard rather than through the usual terminal. She was headed in the wrong direction, to Cheyenne, Wyoming, as a precaution, and Ray Humphreys stated that he was most fearful during that time when they had a one-and-a-half-hour layover waiting for the next train. Josephine arrived safely in San Diego and was greeted by her distraught family.

AUTHOR'S PERSPECTIVE

When speaking to my cousin about her mother, Josie, being extradited to Colorado, she told me that she was unaware of the entire event. She was a teenager at the time and was not informed why her mother left her siblings and herself. She also said that Josie and Anna Piscopo's (Danna) families were very close growing up after their father's deaths.

My uncle Pete looked so cute as a young boy in the *Rocky Mountain News* photo with his mother, Jennie. I find it funny that this three-year-old was to be the only one of Pete Carlino's boys who was ever in jail. Peter II accompanied his mother in the Denver jail for two days.

Chapter 19

"Ingiustizia"

INJUSTICE

Josephine's timing to return to San Diego couldn't have been better. A gangland war had started up again and diverted resources that could have been used against her as gangsters were fighting another turf war over bootleg territories. A week of violence and indictments rocked the Denver underworld as James Curcio was shot and wounded on March 15.[176] Two days later, Vincent Mortellaro was killed, and former Carlino associates Joe Borrello and Frank Mortellaro were wounded along with Roxie Stone in North Denver.[177] One day after the shooting, Denver police chief Albert T. Clarke made an announcement that all suspected bootleggers would be arrested for vagrancy.[178] By Saturday, Chief Clarke had made good on his promise and had forty gangster suspects in jail, as well as one of Roma's henchmen.[179] On Sunday, the credible death threats began again against Wettengel and his staff as they prepared for the Bruno Mauro trial, as well as the indictment of Joe Roma for the attempted murder of Lawrence Baldesareli.[180] By the end of the week, Roma's brother-in-law, Frank Greco, had been arrested with two charges against him.[181]

The Mauro trial was inching closer, and Roma was fighting a war on two fronts. Rival gangs were challenging him for his territory in Denver, and he was at the center of two high-profile court cases. The Bruno Mauro trial was scheduled to begin on April 11, 1932 (one year to the day from when Baldesareli was gunned down in front of the Mayflower Hotel). D.A. Wettengel stated that the prosecution planned to have Josephine Carlino brought back to testify in the trial and that special precautions were going

 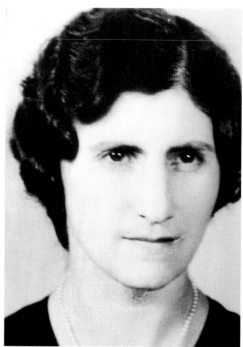

Left: District Attorney Earl Wettengel. *Courtesy of the Carlino family collection.*

Right: Jennie Carlino. *Courtesy of the Carlino family collection.*

to be made to ensure her safety.[182] On April 11, the deputy district attorney petitioned Judge McDonough for a continuance because Josephine Carlino would not be able to make it back to Denver in time for the trial. Mauro attorney Mahoney offered no objection, and the trial was rescheduled for April 25, 1932. The Colletti brothers were still missing and presumed to be hidden in cities back east.[183] Wettengel made a change to his previous statement on April 11 and said that Josephine Carlino would be excused from testifying at the trial—her deposition she gave in March would be used in the proceedings.[184]

Jury selection began on April 25, and the prosecution announced that it would show the movie that was filmed the day of the murder and show the autopsy footage as well.[185] One juror was excused when he told the court that he had known Joe Roma for six months and sold him a stove.[186] A complete list of the twelve jurors was posted in the *Rocky Mountain News*, as were their addresses and professions.

Without Josephine Carlino or Jimmie Colletti present to testify, Jennie Carlino was the state's star witness. She testified, but her testimony was as beneficial to the defense as it was for the prosecution. She stated that she had seen Mauro in the house and spoken to him but that he paid little attention to her; also, she had seen a suspicious man walking back and forth in front of Sam Carlino's house just before the murder. J.D. Taylor, who lived one block away from Sam's house, testified that he had seen the suspicious man as well. George Pratt, who lived at 1244 California Street, said he saw a man running from the house about a minute after the shooting but could not identify him. Next-door neighbor J.B. Newman told of Jimmie Colletti coming to her window motioning for help, and when she arrived, she saw Josephine sprawled over her dead husband's body with blood smeared on her face. Mrs. J. Crette and Mrs. Lydia McAvoy both testified that they had heard gunshots in the Carlino home.[187]

Defense attorney Charles T. Mahoney sprang a surprise by calling Bruno Mauro as his only witness. "I didn't kill Sam Carlino," stated Mauro on the witness stand. "He was my boss....I ran a still for him near Central City and I liked him." He stated that he was in the home prior to the killing but had left before the shooting began. He stated that he saw two men outside the home—one in a black leather coat and black hat and another on the corner in a gray sweater, a cap and blue trousers. He continued, "I didn't know either of them....I turned and looked back and saw the man with the cap going into the gate at the Carlino house....Then I got a streetcar and met a man, Joe Picoli. He had brought me up from Pueblo that morning on a load of liquor. I met him at the garage. He had delivered the load and took me back to Pueblo. We got to Pueblo about dinner time and I saw in the papers that Sam had been killed and they accused me of it....I knew with Sam being killed they would get other members of the gang. That meant they would get me too. So I went away."

Mauro admitted to running a whiskey still for Sam, that he was paid $125 per month and that he was going to take the fall for accepting responsibility of the still when he was arrested with Joe Ferraro. He said he was at the Carlino home to discuss his case with Sam and that he was told that he was not going to be tried right away. Mauro told Sam to reach him by telephone at his aunt's house. When asked if he shot Sam Carlino, he snapped, "No sir."[188]

The defense was based on the theory that the unidentified man walking back and forth in front of the Carlino home and an accomplice were the real killers. Mahoney said that they were imported gunmen brought in

Joe Carlino, Pete Carlino Jr., Chuck Carlino and Sammy Carlino (the author's father), 1932. *Courtesy of the Carlino family collection.*

Victor Carlino and the infamous 1929 Dodge Senior sedan, 1932. *Courtesy of the Carlino family collection.*

from out of town to kill Carlino. The defense rested, and Mauro's fate was in the hands of the jury.

The case went to jury at 8:30 p.m., and the first ballot voted came back 11–1. Two hours later, at 10:20 p.m., all twelve jurors found Bruno Mauro not guilty of the murder of Sam Carlino. Immediately after he was acquitted, Mauro was arrested for possession of a whiskey still. He pleaded guilty. One week later, he was sentenced to four years at the Chillicothe Federal Reformatory and fined $1,000.

On June 4, 1932, Jennie Carlino's suit against the Potomac and the Homestead Insurance Companies was dismissed. A settlement had been reached, but the amount was not revealed. Unknown to the public was that the Muro couple had received $4,000 for payment on the mortgage and Jennie received nothing—at least, nothing but relief that her debt to the Muros had been paid.[189]

Throughout 1932, Denver had become the epicenter of gangland violence. The Carlino brothers were gone, and the power vacuum that existed after their exit was being felt by Joe Roma. He was being challenged by his enemies and was beginning to lose respect among his crew. One of Pete Carlino's teenage boys vowed an oath of revenge against the murderers responsible for his father's death. Shortly after that vendetta was declared, Jennie Carlino was notified that she and her six boys should be out of Colorado within twenty-four hours or they all would be killed. This was motivation enough for them to pack everything they could fit in their 1929 Dodge Senior sedan and escape to California. No vendetta was ever enacted.

Conclusion

Pete and Sam Carlino's story was truly "stranger than a movie thriller" and added to the annals of the history of organized crime. The connections between Pellegrino Scaglia, Nicola Gentile and the Carlino brothers prove that there was an organized leadership of mafia-run cities reaching as far west as Pueblo, Colorado, in 1922. The tracking of Pete Carlino's movements on his way to the East Coast by authorities demonstrated law enforcement's ability to keep tabs on high-profile characters but not necessarily understand the immensity of the organization. The June 24, 1931 article in the *Rocky Mountain News* confirmed Pete's movements back east and reported his meeting with the recognized leader of the mafia, Salvatore Maranzano. A link that had never been made that connected Pete Carlino and the New York mob was now established.

When I began researching for this book, I scoured the Internet for anything about my grandfather and his associates. I found dozens of authentic historic photographs that were used in the original articles, and I purchased them online. I located two editions of the *Rocky Mountain News* from June 1931 that were for sale on eBay. One had an impressive headline, included as a photo in this book, and another was so fragile I was afraid to unfold the crumbling brown paper that was nearly ninety years old. Once I began the chapters on Pete's capture and death, I amassed all of my research, read over them thoroughly and made detailed notes. I remembered that I had purchased an original newspaper and had not read the article completely. I carefully placed the crumbling paper on the floor and took high-resolution photographs of each side of the article. After cropping the articles I finally read them in their entirety and was completely astounded at what I had found. The missing piece to the puzzle had been stored in my closet for the past eight years until I discovered it while writing the final chapters.

I always knew that there was an affiliation with Maranzano, but I could never prove it until now. Whether Luciano gave the go-ahead for Roma to kill Pete is another question, but I truly believe that a connection between Carlino and Maranzano has been established. Pete's friend Paul Danna, who supplied alibi testimony for him in 1926, had moved to New York and was living in the same house as Salvatore Maranzano's brother and nephew at 93 Truxton Street in Brooklyn. Was it a coincidence that Pete was murdered at the same time Maranzano and his lieutenants were eliminated? Maybe, maybe not. But the *Rocky Mountain News* article of June 24, 1931, has made a connection between Colorado and New York that had never been established before.

Pete Carlino's cousin Joe Petralia set him up to be killed by Joe Roma's associates. I had been told by my father, Sam, that Petralia was responsible for setting Pete up to be killed, and the letters that were found on Roma at the time of his death substantiate my father's claims. Why would Joe Petralia expect a favor from Joe Roma while he was in prison unless he had done something very significant to earn it? A question that is still unanswered is why Joe Roma decided to have Pete Carlino killed on September 10, 1931, when Roma had been instructed that Pete was to remain unharmed?

Author and mafia historian Thomas Hunt had an interesting theory. He wondered if Pete Carlino's murder had been sanctioned by Salvatore Maranzano and that maybe Carlino was part of Maranzano's planned nationwide purge of mafia chieftains across the country. Luciano and Lansky eliminated Maranzano before his plan of killing his rivals went into effect. Pete's plan to visit Joe Petralia at the Canon City Penitentiary was set up days in advance of his murder. Lucky Luciano would not have tipped his hand and authorized a murder outside the New York area before he knew that Maranzano was no longer a threat.

After pondering Tom's theory, I am inclined to agree with him. Roma getting the order to kill Pete from Maranzano and not from Luciano makes more sense. Maranzano had planned the purging of all of his rivals, but the plan never got fully enacted. Luciano and Lansky killed him first.

Movies have portrayed the mafia as a romantic, honorable secret society full of intrigue. The truth is that there is no honor among thieves, and

Joe Carlino, Aunt Josephine Carlino, Peter Carlino Jr., Vic Carlino and Sam Carlino (the author's father). *Courtesy of the Carlino family collection.*

these men would sell out to the highest bidder once a better opportunity arose. The romantic notion that these men wouldn't change their allegiance is ludicrous. Most gangsters have shown that once faced with the threat of death or incarceration, they will often do anything to save their skins. Government informants have been the greatest tool law enforcement has had to help put away these criminals.

Pete Carlino's boys would have grown up in a world of crime if he had not been killed in 1931. Sam and Pete Carlino both died of "natural causes"—natural to the line of work they chose. The Carlino brothers' decisions led them down a bloody path that proved that their fate was inevitable. All four of Vito Carlino's sons died of gunshot wounds, and

Gangsters' playful side. Pete Carlino, Rudy Constantino, Josie Carlino, Jennie Carlino, Sam Carlino (with snowball) and Joe Petralia, January 1931. *Courtesy of the Carlino family collection.*

thirteen children were fatherless. Whatever misgivings Pete had as a human being, there was a glimpse of humanity he had as a father. All six of his boys led honest, hardworking, patriotic lives. My dad, Sam, and his brothers Steve and Pete Jr. were raised by their older brother Joe. After their mother died of stomach cancer in 1935, the six boys of Pete and Jennie Carlino vowed to stick together forever. The brothers opened a fruit and vegetable stand on Monterey Highway in San Jose in 1938 and later the Time Market, an Italian grocery store in 1950. Their strength in numbers would help ensure not only their success in business but also their safety from the men who had killed their father. The vendetta that was declared in 1932 was taken seriously enough that the five remaining brothers were "checked up on" every few years throughout the 1950s and 1960s to ensure that they were not regrouping or would pose a threat to the Colorado Mafia. The Carlino boys would be respected members of the San Jose community and continue to quietly give to charity throughout their lives. Many families were affected by their generosity.

Pete and Sam's children would remain close throughout their lives, but the next generation of Carlinos would lose touch with their cousins who were separated by four hundred miles. In San Diego, I attended two family reunions in 1985 and 1986 and had a chance to visit with my dad's first cousins and see a unique bond that time and distance could not separate. I cannot imagine going through what those children endured in that desperate era. I must reiterate that I am so proud that all six of Pete and Jennie's boys never had criminal records and that when their father died, it turned the brothers 180 degrees from their certain path of depravation. All six boys were respected in their community, and the tragic loss of brother Steve in 1941 in Oahu, Hawaii, brought the five remaining brothers even closer. The brothers would eventually separate as partners after thirty years in business together, but their children would remain close as cousins to this day. Pete and Sam Carlino led a notorious life in an era that created organized crime, and their infamous history will be recollected for years to come.

Appendix I

The Players

FRANK BACINO—Danna brothers associate. He was the Pueblo distributor of Danna liquor. He resupplied Dannas with ammo during Baxter Bridge Shootout. He was killed by niece Rose Piscopo and her brother, James Giarratano, in Denver in 1926.

LAWRENCE BALDESARELI—Federal undercover agent who infiltrated the Carlino gang to expose and help topple their empire. He was shot and wounded on April 11, 1931.

JOE BONANNO—Underling to Salvatore Maranzano. He would become boss after Maranzano's murder on September 10, 1931.

JOE BORRELLO (BARRY)—Carlino associate. He was caught with Pete and Sam at the "Bootleggers Convention." He was shot and wounded on several occasions.

CHARLIE CARLINO—Pete and Sam's younger brother, killed by John and Pete Danna and crew at the Baxter Bridge Shootout on September 10, 1923.

JENNIE CARLINO—Pete Carlino's wife, mother of six boys. She fled Colorado to California with twenty-four hours' notice in 1932. She died in 1935 of stomach cancer.

JOSEPHINE CARLINO—Sam Carlino's wife. She was sister to Anna (Piscopo) Danna. She was extradited from California to testify in trial of Bruno Mauro for husband Sam's murder.

PETE CARLINO—Boss of the Carlino faction that ruled Southern Colorado and tried to muscle in on the Denver bootleg territory. He was found shot dead on a secluded road outside Pueblo on September 10, 1931.

SAM CARLINO—Underboss to brother Pete. He was shot in the back by employee Bruno Mauro on May 8, 1931.

STEFANO CARLINO—Pete and Sam's older brother. He arrived in 1898 from Sicily at fifteen years old. He sold real estate and insurance and was a notary public. He was murdered in Manhattan, New York, in August 1918.

VITO CARLINO—Father to Steve, Pete, Sam and Charlie Carlino. All four of his sons would be killed by gunshot.

RALPH CARR—U.S. attorney for Colorado. He recruited Lawrence Baldesareli to search for Dale Kearney's murderer and placed Baldesareli into position to infiltrate the Carlino gang.

GUISEPPE CEFALU—Sam Cefalu's father. He put up bond with Joe Roma to bail Pete Carlino out of jail in June 1931. His daughter Francis Cefalu married Eugene Smaldone.

SAM CEFALU—Carlino associate. He was caught protecting fifty-five kegs of Carlino whiskey with Sam Carlino and Charlie Mauro in 1929.

JOHN CHA—Ran a store in Trinidad that peddled Carlino booze. Carlino Associate. Cha and his wife disappeared in February 1931 but were found alive in April living in Los Angeles, California. He was mayor of Trinidad, Colorado, during the early 1960s.

DAN COLLETTI—Convicted arsonist who played part in explosion of Pete Carlino's house. He changed his last name to Collette and moved to Los Angeles. He died on February 22, 1956, of a heart attack. He was cousin to Pete Carlino.

JIMMIE COLLETTI—Shot and wounded when Sam Carlino was killed by Bruno Mauro. He was stepbrother to Dan Colletti. He changed his name back to its original form, Vincenzo James Amore Jr. He died on December 7, 1985.

RUDY CONSTANTINO—Born Pete Carlino, son of Paul Carlino. He was wanted for murder and changed his name to Rudy Constantino in 1929. He was Pete Carlino's first cousin.

LUCILLE CRUPI—Associated with Milwaukee mob figures during the 1920s and 1930s. She gave interview with the Milwaukee police on June 3, 1931, verifying that Pete Carlino was in Milwaukee in late May 1931.

JOHN DANNA—Patriarch of the Danna family, rival bootleggers to the Carlinos. He was killed by Carlo Marino Jr. in 1925 over a water rights dispute.

PAUL DANNA—Friend of Pete and Sam Carlino. He gave alibi testimony for Pete to the police just hours after the Danna brothers' murders. He also took the stand in the trial in Pete's favor in the murder of his cousins Tony and Pete Danna in 1926. In 1930, he lived in the same house as Salvatore Maranzano's brother and son in Brooklyn, New York.

PETE DANNA—Rival bootlegger to the Carlinos. He married Anna Piscopo, which made him Sam Carlino's brother-in-law. He was shot dead on Pueblo Street with his brother Tony by the Carlino faction in 1926.

SAM DANNA—Youngest of Danna brothers. He witnessed his brothers killed on Pueblo Street in 1926. He was shot and wounded in 1928 on his farm and was shot again and killed in 1930 in downtown Pueblo.

TONY DANNA—Rival bootlegger to the Carlinos. He was shot dead on Pueblo Street with his brother Pete in 1926.

SAM ENGLISH (INGLESE)—Pueblo saloon operator. He owned the Monte Carlo Pool Hall. He was wounded when speaking to the Danna brothers at the time of their slaying in front of his establishment in 1926.

JOE FERRARO—Nephew to Carlinos through Steve's wife, Anna Ferraro. Two trunks containing Carlino heirlooms were found at his home after the bombing of Pete Carlino's house. He was wanted in connection with the bombing.

NICOLA GENTILE—Mafia boss from Kansas City, deported in 1938 to Sicily. He wrote the book *Vita di Capomafia* in 1963, a memoir in which he described the aftermath of Pellegrino Scaglia's murder and other significant mafia events during the 1920s and the 1930s.

JAMES GIARRATANO—Convicted to life in prison for killing his sister's uncle Frank Bacino. He was sought in Carl Mulay's assassination attempt but released.

CHARLIE GUARDAMONDO—Pete Carlino was arrested on Charlie's ranch on June 18, 1931. He was cousin to Pete Carlino.

DALE KEARNEY—Federal Bureau of Prohibition agent responsible for numerous arrests. He was gunned down in cold blood on July 6, 1930, in Aguilar, Colorado. This was the catalyst for the Bureau of Prohibition to send Lawrence Baldesareli to investigate his unsolved murder.

CHARLES "LUCKY" LUCIANO (BORN SALVATORE LUCANIA)—New York Mafia underboss to Joe Masseria. He orchestrated Masseria's murder in April 1931. Five months later, with Meyer Lansky, he orchestrated Salvatore Maranzano's murder.

SALVATORE MARANZANO—Self-proclaimed *capo dei capi*, mafia boss in New York. He organized a nationwide meeting in May 1931 at Hotel Congress in Chicago hosted by Al Capone. He was killed on September 10, 1931.

CARLO MARINO JR.—Shot and killed John Danna on his farm in 1925 after a dispute over water rights and a grievous insult to his father. He disappeared to New Orleans until he returned to Pueblo in 1927.

BRUNO MAURO—Carlino whiskey still operator. He killed Sam Carlino and wounded Jimmie Colletti on orders from Joe Roma.

CARL MULAY—Pete Carlino's brother-in-law. He was married to Jennie's sister Catherine. He was a lieutenant in the Carlino faction.

JOHN MULAY—Older brother to Carl Mulay. He owned the American Pool Hall in Pueblo, distributor of Carlino booze. He was shot and killed on the street by the Danna faction in Pueblo in 1923.

CHRIS MURKURI—"Dynamite Chris," convicted arsonist for several fires. He managed the bombing of Pete Carlino's Federal Boulevard home. He was arrested for arson just after being released from prison for the Carlino fire.

JOE PETRALIA—Pete Carlino's cousin. He was convicted for arson in his part of blowing up Pete's house. He tipped Joe Roma to Pete Carlino's whereabouts from jail, precipitating his murder.

JOE PISCOPO—Sought for murder of Vincenzo Urso and attempted murder of Carl Mulay. He was shot and killed on his porch on July 3, 1924, by Carlino-hired gunmen.

ROSE PISCOPO—Joe Piscopo's widow. He plotted with brother James Giarratano to kill her uncle Frank Bacino in 1926.

CHIEF RICHARD REED—Corrupt police chief appointed by Mayor Stapleton. He always wore his giant, infamous diamond ring and drove a luxury Packard on a meager police chief's salary. He was nicknamed "Diamond Dick" Reed.

JOE ROMA—Denver mob boss and onetime friend to the Carlinos. He would eventually orchestrate Sam and Pete's murders in 1931 before his own slaying in 1933.

PELLEGRINO SCAGLIA (TONY VIOLA)—Pueblo mafia chieftain and distributor of Carlino booze at time of his murder in 1922. He was slain while riding in a wagon with two young children. His wife, Maria, was godmother to Pete Carlino's son Joe.

JOE SPINUZZI—Enforcer and bodyguard for Danna brothers. He was killed by three of the Carlino crew outside the Pizzutti Roadhouse in 1926.

BEN STAPLETON—Denver mayor, member of the Ku Klux Klan and a crooked politician. Stapleton Airport in Denver was named after him.

IGNAZIO VACCARO—Pete Carlino's cousin, bodyguard and lieutenant. He was last seen on February 18, 1931. He is presumed murdered, and his body was likely burned in a furnace.

PIETRINA VACCARO—Wife of Ignazio Vaccaro. After her husband's death, she would marry Jennie Riggio's brother Charlie.

EARL WETTENGEL—District attorney who prosecuted Pete Carlino and crew, as well as Joe Roma and crew.

Josephine Carlino's Spaghetti Sauce Recipe

This is the sauce that was served from my mom's kitchen since I was a child. Aunt Josie showed her how to make it. My friends still talk about eating spaghetti and ravioli at my house and how they loved my mom's real *spaghetti sauce. Use liberally over linguine, spaghetti, ravioli or your favorite pasta.* Mangia!

2 pounds Italian sausage
3 tablespoons olive oil
3 yellow onions, diced ¼- to ½-inch thick
1 ½ pounds mushrooms, sliced (Crimini or white)
16 whole cloves of fresh peeled garlic, chopped fine
2 28-ounce cans tomato puree
2 6-ounce cans tomato paste (once emptied, use warm water to extract all the paste residue from can)
12 ounces dry red wine (half bottle)
1 28-ounce can of water
16 fresh basil leaves, chopped
3 sprigs of fresh oregano (leaves removed from stem and chopped)
6 tablespoons sugar (add more if desired)
1 tablespoon salt (kosher or sea salt preferred)
1 tablespoon black pepper
½ teaspoon crushed red pepper

In a large pot, brown the Italian sausage until the sausage grease coats the bottom of pan (the sausage will almost be done but not quite). Remove sausage to plate.

Add olive oil to sausage grease and sauté onions, mushrooms and garlic until onions are translucent and mushrooms are cooked.

Add tomato puree, tomato paste, red wine, water, basil, oregano, sugar, salt, pepper and crushed red pepper to pot. Let simmer uncovered on low for 1 hour and then put Italian sausage back into pot. Simmer at least 2 more hours. If sauce is too watery, just simmer for longer uncovered. Don't forget to stir it.

Aunt Josephine Carlino with Sam Carlino (author), 1967. *Courtesy of the Carlino family collection.*

Notes

Chapter 2

1. New Orleans passenger list, 1920–45, Ancestry.com.
2. Italian Side, genealogy in Lucca Sicula, www.italianside.com.
3. Find A Grave, Vito Carlino, 2-18-1853–11-6-1912, www.findagrave.com.
4. State of New York Bureau of Records, Certificate of Death, August 29, 1918.
5. Ballotpedia, Colorado statewide prohibition measure no. 2, 1914, www.ballotpedia.org.
6. Family Search, Giovanni Danna, www.familysearch.org.
7. Vito Danna, New York passenger arrival list, Ellis Island, 1892–1924, Family Search, www.familysearch.org.
8. Antonio Danna, New York passenger arrival list, Ellis Island, 1892–1924, Family Search, www.familysearch.org.

Chapter 3

9. Humbert S. Nelli, *The Business of Crime* (Chicago: University of Chicago Press, 1976), 98.
10. *America* magazine, "How Dry We Were: Ken Burns and Lynn Novick Revisit Prohibition," www.americanmagazine.org.

11. The State Historical Society of Missouri, "Carry A. Nation, 1846–1911," www.shsmo.org.
12. *Smithsonian* magazine, "Why the Ku Klux Klan Flourished Under Prohibition," www.smithsonianmag.com.
13. U.S. Census 1920, Crowley County.
14. Joanne West Dodd, *Pueblo: A Pictorial History* (Norfolk, VA: Donning Company, 1982).

Chapter 4

15. *The (NY) Sun*, "Say He's Cardinelli Slayer," September 1, 1911, 2.
16. *St. Louis Star and Times*, "Blackhand Feud Shown by Murder Arrest," August 4, 1911, 1.
17. *St. Louis Post-Dispatch*, "Detectives Rush a Murder Suspect Out of Missouri," August 30, 1911, 3.
18. Pueblo City Directories, 1822–1995, Pueblo, Colorado, 1916.
19. United States Department of Justice, FBI Denver Office, Paul E. Bush, investigator, March 23, 1964, re: La Cosa Nostra.
20. Colorado Fuel and Iron Company Records, 1887–1979, Ancestry.com.
21. FBI investigation on Pellegrino Scaglia, Anna Marie Scaglia's birth certificate, March 3, 1964.
22. *Denver Post*, "Anthony Viola, 50 and Frank Cordero, 11, Shot Down While in Grocery Wagon, Are Believed Victims of Italian Feudists," May, 6, 1922, 6.
23. United States Department of Justice, FBI Denver Office, Paul E. Bush, investigator, March 23, 1964, re: La Cosa Nostra.
24. *Pueblo Chieftain*, "Imported Mafia Gunmen Brot Here to Await at Trial of Danna Slayers," September 4, 1926, 2.
25. "Nick Gentile," *Background and History of the Castellammarese War and Early Decades of Organized Crime in America*, translated transcription of the life of Nicolo Gentile (Palermo, Sicily, 1947, 1963), 57, 58, 59, 60.
26. Federal Bureau of Investigation, La Cosa Nostra, Kansas City Division, SA George F. Lueckenhoff, June 8, 1964, AR Conspiracy, 26.
27. Ibid., 28.
28. Jerry Capeci, *The Complete Idiot's Guide to the Mafia* (New York: Alpha Books, n.d.), Part 5, "Mafia Speak," 278.
29. FBI report no. Dn92-222, July 20, 1964, Paul E. Bush, investigator.

Chapter 5

30. *Denver Post*, "Jealous Pueblo Italian Shoots Countryman," February 11, 1903, 7.
31. *Denver Post*, "Three Men Charged with Padding Payroll," June 20, 1912, 1.
32. *Denver Post*, "7 Italians Battle with Revolvers in Pueblo Street," March 1, 1915, 7.
33. Pueblo, Colorado directory, 1916, Ancestry.com.
34. Pueblo, Colorado directory, "Soft Drinks," Ancestry.com.
35. Pueblo, Colorado directory, "Billiard Hall," Ancestry.com.
36. *Pueblo Chieftain*, "John Mulay Is Killed by Men in Automobile," February 28, 1923.
37. *Pueblo Chieftain*, "One Arrest in Connection with Tuesday Night Slaying," June 22, 1923.
38. *Pueblo Chieftain*, "Jury Unable to Name Man," July 3, 1923.

Chapter 6

39. *Pueblo Chieftain*, "Danno [*sic*] Grilled by Attorneys," December 13, 1923.
40. Haunted Colorado, "Colorado Ghost Tours—Pueblo," www.hauntedcolorado.net.
41. *Lincoln Star*, "Two Dead in a Gun Battle," September 11, 1923, 1.
42. U.S. Census, 1920, "Dominick Inge" (Ingo), Chicago, Illinois.
43. *Arizona Daily Star*, September 11, 1923, 1.
44. *Pueblo Chieftain*, "Danno [*sic*] Case in Hands of Jury," December 15, 1923.
45. *Pueblo Chieftain*, "Jury Is Unable to Agree on Verdict in Danno [*sic*] Case, Dismissed by Judge," December 16, 1923.

Chapter 7

46. U.S. City Directories, 1822–1995, Trinidad, Colorado, 1924.
47. *Pueblo Chieftain*, "Murder Trial," March 3, 1925, 1.
48. *Pueblo Chieftain*, "Murder Trial Here Continues After One Juror Becomes Ill," March 5, 1925.

49. *Pueblo Chieftain*, "Lucia Now," March 3, 1925, 1.

50. *Pueblo Chieftain*, "Black Hand Claims Another Victim in Little Italy Here," July 4, 1924.

51. *Arizona Republic*, "Two Held on Dry Charges," May 1, 1925, 1.

52. Dick Kreck, *Smaldone: The Untold Story of an American Crime Family* (Golden, CO: Fulcrum Publishing, 2009), 60.

53. *Pueblo Chieftain*, "Tragedy Follows Water Rights Dispute," May 2, 1925.

54. *Albuquerque Journal*, "Relative of Man Sought for Crime Shot from Ambush," July 18, 1925.

55. *Santa Ana Register*, "New Chapter Is Written in Feud," May 15, 1927.

56. *Havre Daily News*, "Fear Renewal of Black Hand War in Death of Denver Man," April 15, 1926, 1.

57. *Anaconda Standard*, "Woman Murdered Uncle to Escape His Love Making," April 16, 1926.

58. *Billings (MT) Gazette*, "Woman Says Relative Hounded Her; Others Suggested Slaying Him through Window So She Did; Collapses When Confronted by Brother of Victim," April 16, 1926.

59. *Billings (MT) Gazette*, "Coroners Jury Rejects Woman's Guilt Admission," April 18, 1926.

60. *Arizona Republic*, "Giarratano Is Given Life for Slaying Uncle," October 2, 1926.

61. *Albuquerque (NM) Journal*, "Life Sentence Given Italian Who Killed Man," November 21, 1926, 2.

62. *Independent Record* (Helena, MT), "For His Part in Sending Murderer to a Cell for Life," November 21, 1926.

Chapter 8

63. *Denver Post*, "Sam English Is Latest Reform 'Goat,' at Pueblo," March 8, 1910.

64. *Denver Rocky Mountain News*, "Pueblo Man Asks for $35,500 Damages for False Arrest," March 3, 1921.

65. *Albuquerque Journal*, "Blackhand Is Blamed for a Pueblo Murder," May 15, 1926, 1.

66. *Albuquerque Journal*, "Posse Narrowly Fails to Catch Two of Murder Band at Pueblo," May 17, 1926.

67. *Arizona Republic*, "News Censorship Threats Made Against Newspapers in Blackhand Slaying," May 18, 1926, 2.

68. *Arizona Daily Star*, "Posse Closing on Hunted Men, Says Late Word," May 17, 1926, 1.
69. *Pueblo Chieftain*, "Double Funeral Held for Danna Brothers," May 18, 1926, 1.
70. *Arizona Daily Star*, "Howling Dog Saves Man from Brother's Fate," June 7, 1926, 1.

Chapter 9

71. *Arizona Republic*, "Colorado Governor Offers Reward in Blackhand Death," August 2, 1926, 11.
72. *Anaconda Standard*, "Three of Accused Slayers Surrender," August 23, 1926, 1.
73. *Albuquerque Journal*, "Not Guilty Is Verdict in Murder Case of Three Sicilians," November 22, 1926, 5.
74. *Pueblo Chieftain*, "Imported Mafia Gunmen Brot Here," 1.
75. *Santa Fe New Mexican*, "Danna Trial On in Pueblo, Colo.," November 9, 1926, 2.
76. *Arizona Republic*, "Colorado Judge Orders 13 Men on Murder Jury," November 11, 1926, 10.
77. Ibid.
78. *Santa Fe New Mexican*, "Danna Trial on in Pueblo, Colo.," November 9, 1926, 2.
79. *Albuquerque Journal*, "Life Sentence Given Italian Who Killed Man," November 21, 1926, 2.
80. *Arizona Daily Star*, "Not Guilty Is Verdict After 16 Hour Fight," November 22, 1926, 2.

Chapter 10

81. *Albuquerque Journal*, "Guard Hospital," October 16, 1928.
82. *Denver Rocky Mountain News*, "Boys Deny Taking Horses from Pueblo Ranchman," July 16, 1916, 8.
83. *Denver Post*, "Suspect Confesses Two Post Office Robberies in State," October 18, 1922.
84. *Denver Post*, "Pueblo Youth Held, Alleged to Have Tried Safe Robbery," February 28, 1922, 19.

85. *Albuquerque Journal*, "Murdered Wife Named Slayers Before Dying; Both Missing," April 13, 1929, 1.

86. *Montana Standard*, "Bullet-Riddled Bodies of Pair Found Yesterday," April 11, 1929, 8.

87. *Albuquerque Journal*, "Missing Pueblo Girl Abducted to New Mexico," July 26, 1927.

88. *Montana Standard*, "Brothers Are Held for Death of Pair," April 15, 1929, 16.

89. *Denver Rocky Mountain News*, "Killing of Last Danna Brother Defies Solution," May 8, 1930, 9.

Chapter 11

90. Josie Carlino, *The Carlino Family Cookbook*, comp. Josie Carlino (Olathe, KS: Cookbook Publishers, 1989), 43.

91. *Denver Post*, "Dry Agents Seize Rum-Laden Truck on Way to Denver," March 7, 1929, 12.

92. *Omaha World Herald*, "Dry Agents Killed After a Daring Series of Raids," July 7, 1930, 1.

93. *St. Louis Star*, "Raiding Dry Agent Trapped and Shot to Death on Road," July 7, 1930, 7.

94. *Las Vegas (NM) Daily Optic*, "Colorado Dry Officer Slain from Ambush," July 9, 1930, 6.

95. *Great Falls (MT) Tribune*, "Joints Locked After Dry Slain," July 16, 1930, 2.

96. *Denver Rocky Mountain News*, "Inside Stories of Carlino Fire Told," May 12, 1931, 2.

97. *Denver Post*, "U.S. Plans to Prosecute Jailed Men," January 26, 1931, 1.

98. *Denver Post*, "Police Records Show How Bootleggers Are Saved by Political Pull," January 27, 1931, 1.

99. Ibid.

100. *Greeley (CO) Daily Tribune*, "Ike Merritt's Charges to Be Investigated," July 7, 1931.

101. *Denver Post*, "Gamblers Pay City Officials for Protection, Says Merritt," February 20, 1931, 1.

102. History Colorado, KKK membership, Denver, Colorado.

Chapter 12

103. *Denver Post*, "Detectives Are Ordered to Jail All Bootleggers," February 20, 1931, 1, 3.

104. *Denver Post*, "Two Who Disappeared with Vaccaro Found Alive on the Coast," April 12, 1931, 3.

105. *Denver Rocky Mountain News*, "Inside Stories of Carlino Fire Told," May 12, 1931, 1, 2.

106. *San Bernardino (CA) Sun*, "Mysterious Fire Investigation Reopened with Arrest in Denver," April 16, 1931, 13.

107. *Denver Rocky Mountain News*, "Inside Stories of Carlino Fire Told," May 12, 1931, 1, 2.

108. *Denver Post*, "Neighbors Say Gang Blocked Alley with Their Liquor Trucks," March 18, 1931, 1.

109. *Denver Post*, "Conferences Held to Compile List of Denver Public Enemies," March 19, 1931, 4.

110. *Denver Post*, "Police Seize Trunks in Hunt for Carlino," March 20, 1931, 10.

111. *Denver Post*, "Police Seize Guns and Jail Sam Carlino," March 21, 1931, 1.

112. Ibid., 1, 3.

113. *Denver Post*, "Federal Agent Posing as Gangster," April 11, 1931, 3.

114. *Denver Post*, "Six Will Face Plot Charge in Carlino Blast," March 23, 1931, 1, 4.

115. *Denver Post*, "Court Waits Over an Hour for Carlino Gang," March 28, 1931, 2.

Chapter 13

116. *Denver Post*, "Two Men in Car Fire Shotgun at Victim in Front of Hotel," April 11, 1931, 1, 3.

117. *Denver Post*, "Baldesareli Is Seeker of Adventure in Fight Against Underworld," April 11, 1931, 3.

118. *Denver Post*, "Two Who Disappeared with Vaccaro Found Alive on Coast," April 12, 1931, 3.

119. *Denver Post*, "Four Held in Carlino Blast Will Fight Delay in Trial," April 12, 1931.

120. *Denver Rocky Mountain News*, "Earlier Carlino Fire Is Probed," April 15, 1931.
121. *Clovis News-Journal*, "Bootleg King Is Sued for Damages," April 23, 1931, 1.
122. *Denver Post*, "Heads of Carlino Gang Are Unable to Pay Attorneys," April 22, 1931, 14.

Chapter 14

123. *Oakland (CA) Tribune*, "Gangsters Add Notch to Gun," April 5, 1931, 8.
124. *Denver Post*, "Liquor Hearing for Carlino Gang Postponed," April 29, 1931, 18.
125. *Denver Post*, "State Nearly Ready to Rest in Mauro Case," April 27, 1932, 9.
126. *Denver Rocky Mountain News*, "Fear Garlic-Poisoned Slug Felled Aid of Sam Carlino," May 10, 1931, 2.
127. *Denver Post*, "State Nearly Ready to Rest in Mauro Case," April 27, 1931, 9.
128. *Denver Rocky Mountain News*, "Carlino Broke Unable to Pay Killer Says Chief Reed," May 10, 1931, 2.
129. *Denver Post*, "Pete's Brother Slain When He Attempts to Escape Assassin," May 8, 1931, 3.
130. *Denver Rocky Mountain News*, "Vivid Story Told by Young Victim of Assassin's Gun," May 9, 1931, 1.
131. *Denver Rocky Mountain News*, "Gun Victim Has Hair Combed by Nurse for Photo," May 9, 1931, 1.
132. *Denver Post*, "Officers Learn Joseph Roma Was Wed Only a Few Weeks Ago," May 9, 1931, 5.
133. *New York Times*, "Fired Machine Gun in Ludlow Battle," May 21, 1914.
134. *Denver Rocky Mountain News*, "Denver Gang Data Bared as State Seizes Records," May 9, 1931, 2.
135. *Denver Rocky Mountain News*, "Carlino Gang Split Caused Assassination," May 9, 1931, 2.
136. *Denver Rocky Mountain News*, "Carlino Slain Over Failure to Pay Mauro," May 10, 1931, 2.

Chapter 15

137. Bonanno, *Man of Honor*, 128.
138. *Denver Rocky Mountain News*, "Gang Warfare Is Ended Here," June 24, 1931, 1, 2.
139. Bonanno, *Man of Honor*, 127.
140. *Denver Post*, "Mayor Stapleton Why Did You Permit Arson Blast?" May 13, 1931, 5.
141. *Denver Post*, "You Are On Trial Before Voters for Failure to Do Your Duty," May 13, 1931, 5.
142. *Denver Rocky Mountain News*, "Carlino Gangsters Hear Secrets Told," May 12, 1931, 1.
143. *Denver Rocky Mountain News*, "Fate of Carlino Gang Rests in the Hands of Jury," May 13, 1931, 2.
144. *Denver Rocky Mountain News*, "Police Alert, Attorney Says," May 13, 1931, 3.
145. *Denver Post*, "Liquor Charges Against Carlino Gang Dismissed," May 15, 1931, 3.

Chapter 16

146. *Rocky Mountain Times*, "Gangland Warfare Has Ended Here," June 24, 1931, 1, 2.
147. 1930 U.S. Census, Brooklyn Borough, Nicolo Maranzano, Dominick Maranzano, Paul Danna, 93 Truxton Street, Brooklyn, New York.
148. *Denver Post*, "Alibi Testimony Is Given by Many in Danna Murder," November 18, 1926, 9.
149. Gavin Schmitt, "The Interrogation of Lucille Crupi," in *The Milwaukee Mafia: Mobsters in the Heartland* (Fort Lee, NJ: Barricade Books, 2015), 131–34.
150. Milwaukee police interview with Lucille Crupi, June 3, 1931, in Schmitt, *Milwaukee Mafia*.
151. *Denver Rocky Mountain News*, "Gang Warfare Is Ended Here," 1–2.
152. Bonanno, *Man of Honor*, 128.

Chapter 17

153. *Denver Post*, "Third Member of Carlino Gang Sent to Reformatory," June 12, 1931, 5.

154. David Critchley, *The Origin of Organized Crime in America: The New York City Mafia, 1891–1931* (New York: Routledge, 2009), 195.

155. Gentile, *Background and History*, 111, 112, 113.

156. *Asbury Park (NJ) Evening Press*, "N.J. Racketeers Die in Gang War," September 14, 1931, 2.

157. Peter Maas, *The Valachi Papers* (New York: G.P. Putnam and Sons, 1968), 113.

158. Critchley, *Origin of Organized Crime in America*, 206–7.

159. Nelli, *Business of Crime*, 182–83.

160. *Denver Post*, "Pueblo Police Obtain Clews to Slayers of Pete Carlino," September 15, 1931, 35.

161. *Denver Post*, "Denver Booze Chief Shot from Back by Rival Gangsters," September 14, 1931, 1, 4.

162. *Denver Rocky Mountain News*, "Bullet Ridden Body Is Found Near Pueblo," September 14, 1931, 1.

163. *Denver Post*, "Carlino Assassin's Apparently Employed Poisonous Bullets," September 15, 1931, 11.

164. *Denver Rocky Mountain News*, "Dethroned Gangland King Is Laid to Rest in Denver," September 16, 1931, 1, 2.

165. *Denver Post*, "Roma Letters Link Him with Reign of Crime," February 19, 1933, 3.

Chapter 18

166. *Denver Post*, "North Denver Grocer Freed on $3,000 Bond," February 28, 1931, 1, 3.

167. *Denver Post*, "Youth Accused of Sam Carlino Killing Gives Up," February 24, 1931, 1, 6.

168. *Denver Post*, "North Grocer Freed on $3,000 Bond," February 28, 1931, 1, 3.

169. *Denver Post*, "Sam Carlino Widow Held in California," February 27, 1931, 1, 2.

170. *Denver Post*, "Movies to Show Carlino Murder Scene to Rolph," March 1, 1931, 3.

171. *Denver Post*, "North Denver Grocer Freed on $3,000 Bond," February 28, 1931, 1, 3.

172. *Denver Post*, "Wettengel Receives Death Threats in Carlino Probe," February 29, 1931, 1, 3.

173. *Denver Post*, "Joe Roma Is Indicted in Baldesareli Shooting," March 5, 1932, 1, 3.

174. *Denver Post*, "Sam Carlino Widow Agrees to Tell the Truth of His Death," March 15, 1932, 1, 3.

175. Ibid.

Chapter 19

176. *Denver Post*, "Mystery Shot Wounds Man in Automobile," March 16, 1932, 14.

177. *Denver Post*, "Three Others in Automobile Are Wounded," March 17, 1932, 1.

178. *Denver Post*, "All Suspects Will Be Jailed Whenever Officers See Them," March 18, 1932, 3.

179. *Denver Post*, "Forty Gangster Suspects in Denver Are Jailed," March 19, 1932, 4.

180. *Denver Post*, "Gangsters Threaten to Kill Wettengel and Aids," March 20, 1932, 4.

181. *Denver Post*, "Roma's Brother-in-Law Indicted in Probe of Gangs," March 24, 1932, 3.

182. *Denver Post*, "Bruno Mauro Goes on Trial Monday in Carlino Murder," April 10, 1932, 6.

183. *Denver Post*, "Trial of Mauro on Murder Charge Is Delayed Week," April 11, 1932, 9.

184. *Denver Rocky Mountain News*, "Bruno Mauro Murder Trial Set Tomorrow," April 24, 1932, 10.

185. *Denver Post*, "Plea for Death Penalty Likely in Mauro Case," April 25, 1932, 2.

186. *Denver Rocky Mountain News*, "Carlino Slater Suspect Tried," April 26, 1932, 2.

187. *Denver Post*, "State Nearly Ready to Rest in Mauro Case," April 26, 1932, 9.

188. *Denver Rocky Mountain News*, "Not Guilty Jury Verdict in Mauro's Murder Trial," April 27, 1932, 2.

189. *Denver Post*, "Mrs. Carlino Gets Settlement in Insurance Suit," June 4, 1932, 5.

About the Author

Sam Carlino is the grandson of Pete Carlino. Born and raised in Campbell, California, Sam has been working since the age of twelve. His father, Sam Sr., instilled in him a hard work ethic, a love of family and country and the importance of following through on every task at hand. Sam has been a journeyman butcher; restaurant owner; realtor; TV food show producer, director and host; avid outdoorsman; and amateur mafia historian. Married for more than twenty-five years, Sam lives in San Jose, California, with his wife and two teenage daughters.

Visit us at
www.historypress.com